Melodies at Eventide

by

Rex Lee

First Published in 2016 by The Manuscript Publisher

ISBN: 978-0-9576729-7-0

A CIP Catalogue record for this book is available from the
National Library

Typesetting, page design and layout, cover design by
DocumentsandManuscripts.com

MELODIES AT EVENTIDE

DEDICATION

To my sister, Mairéad.

ACKNOWLEDGEMENTS

I would like to thank the following people for their help and general encouragement throughout this project:

Mairéad Lee, Sean Lee, Eoghan Ryan, Joe Rourke, Marie Rourke, John Burns, Graham Sheppard, Billy Carry, Martin Flanagan, Ned Rispin, Niall O'Riordain, Miriam McKenna and Rose Grimes

And the following people for their assistance by supplying information and comments, for proofreading and general editing:

Danny Cusack, Peter McKevitt, Mark Downes, Noel French and Con O'Sullivan

And lastly, to the following for their help with the design and in the final production stages of the memoir:

Oscar Duggan, Sean Lee, Eoghan Ryan and Jess Olohan.

I would also like to express my deep appreciation to all those people, without whose interest and practical help, this memoir would never have seen the light of day.

Rex Lee
December 2015

FOREWORD

It is truly remarkable that an individual born with a disability at the beginning of World War II, whose parents had been informed in dogmatic fashion by their doctor that their 'unfortunate child would never walk or even talk in any meaningful coherent way' and be destined rather for an institution, would many years later be able declare that he 'had led a privileged existence.' The memoirs of Rex Lee clearly show that by not accepting the established 'medical' approach to disability and, through the very determined quest by his family – particularly his mother and aunt – for him to lead a normal and independent life, this 'privileged existence' was made possible.

Out of desperation was born the motivation to embrace the philosophy of physical and mental compensation: by finding a faculty for the one he lost or never had. In today's lexicon of disability-speak, this is known as the 'social model' and in this regard, Rex can be regarded as a living example of a paradigm-changing pioneer. Rex did not take the path of least resistance and his ability to delight us with entertaining stories serves to bring the abstract to life.

These stories tell us how the challenges of his school days, his time studying horticulture at Knockanally and the friends he made, taught him to regard loyalty and trust to be the highest of virtues and a primary principle that must be observed. His introduction to Macra na Feirme and their debating competitions prepared him well to take up positions at county and national level, with both Macra and the IFA, and subsequently, to represent Macra at international conferences. Looking for 'a meaningful way to real freedom' inspired him to establish his own nursery at home and he quickly also became a leader of the representative bodies for that enterprise.

This pioneering approach directed him towards a pre-university course at the Rehab Group's National Training Centre in Dublin and subsequently, onto UCD for an Arts degree, followed by a Master's Degree in Film Studies. This was a wonderful achievement for anyone, though an even more remarkable outcome in Rex's case. And proof that the principles he lived by could bear fruit – as they did in such a stunning fashion.

Rex is truly the king and subject of his own realm and living proof that, what he termed as 'mental and physical compensation', can overcome most obstacles to leading a normal and independent life. It has in his own words been 'a privileged existence'. Rex masterfully demonstrates that for us.

– **Peter McKevitt** (formerly North Eastern Manager of Rehab Care)

INTRODUCTION

It is strange the way that memories come flooding on top of you with a vividness you had never anticipated, urged on by the recall of random events. A recent *Mooney Goes Wild* programme on RTÉ Radio had Derek Mooney talking about Japanese knotweed, a plant imported from the Far East, which had won several horticultural awards but nevertheless, became a highly invasive weed. For me this brought back a flood of memories regarding other such horticultural disasters. A conifer that became known as Castlewellan Gold was discovered in the North in 1948 but not introduced into the Republic until the 1960s. As I was heavily involved in nursery stock at the time, I became only too familiar with the history of this plant.

But all is not disaster. There are more pleasant memories from my early life – especially of my mother and her sisters, who provided me with a secure and loving background, a vantage point from which I could safely view the world. The way different people viewed disability – whether positively or negatively – also helped me to appreciate the difference between the medical and social models. One of the achievements of my early life was my adoption of, what I came to know as, the Philosophy of Physical and Medical Compensation. Out of desperation was born the motivation to plug that gaping chasm left by disability.

In a way, it has been nothing short of a miracle that I have been able to lead such an independent life. As I have already intimated, this has been in no small part due to the women in my life – my mother and my aunts. In one sense, I have had a privileged existence. Even today, it would be unusual for an able-bodied man to have such an entrée into the sources of power in European affairs and to experience other cultures, notably through a short stint in North America. I am grateful for all this.

Thinking of the story one is about to embark on, one naturally recalls some of the great public events which have occurred in one's lifetime – the fall of the Berlin wall for example, the aftermath of which I witnessed during a sojourn in that city in 1995. Even in this divided city, the great and the universal co-existed with the small and the domestic. What I recall more vividly however, is seaside Skerries of summer 1965; the murmur of the sea at the end of our garden and the tennis court with the long-legged, suntanned girls.

*   *   *

The past is a foreign country. While universally true, this is especially true of the Irish Republic. The Free State, as it became known in the 1920s, had several striking features – one of these was the power of the Catholic Church. This had been so, even before the departure of the British, which led to the creation of two separate, sectarian states: "a Protestant parliament for a Protestant people" in the North and a confessional Catholic state in the South, in conformity with the wishes of its majority.

The North may have had no hesitation in declaring itself a Protestant state; the Free State did not go in for such far-reaching declarations – at least not initially. Nevertheless, as leading politician, Kevin O'Higgins (assassinated in 1927) once declared: he and his colleagues were amongst "the most conservative revolutionaries who ever put through a successful revolution."

Although a special position for the Catholic Church would not be proclaimed until 1937, in the early years of the Free State, all mention of divorce and re-marriage was dropped from the statute book, and some quite draconian censorship legislation was passed into law.

This was the new Ireland of the 1920s, in which my father – along with many others – joined the ranks of the Public Service as a local government official, working in the area of health and welfare. Historically, this particular function of Public Service had developed in three stages: first, the position of Relieving Officer, which emerged just after the Great Famine and under the old Poor Law system; secondly, the position of Home Assistance Officer (that held by my father and other men of his generation), one of the first innovations of the Free State; thirdly, the position of Community Health Officer, which accompanied the establishment of the Health Boards in the 1970s. This final phase would prove very relevant to my own later involvement in community activities but, most particularly, working with and for people with disability.

CONTENTS

Chapter One:
My Family Background

My family's background in Kells, Co. Meath was Edwardian middle-class. This was an age when even the most modest middle-class households had at least one maid and a gardener-cum-handyman. We had, on occasion, two maids and a gardener. It was a seemingly steady and secure background. For us children, it was an ideal life as we resided in a large house, nestled between the town tennis club and an Old IRA man's milking-fields. On balmy summer nights, the strain of a palm court orchestra wafted through the open windows of our bedroom from the tennis club on one side, while the lowing of contented cattle could be heard from the fields on the other. In the fading light, with the evening filled with melodious sounds, we might just discern, on the mantelpiece, the empty jam jars that held the minnows (or pinkeens) we had caught earlier in the day, in a little stream that ran by the end of the garden, past Bolands' cottage and under the Kells-Athboy Road.

We were supposed to catch our minnows by lowering our jam jars, on a length of string, from a parapet wall into the stream. But we learned quite quickly that, by removing our shoes and socks, we could hoover a greater number of minnows by placing the jars a few feet downstream from a large-ish rock, which had shifted slightly. We could then herd our pink and silver harvest into our waiting glass jars.

Boyhood Memory

I vividly recall one particular occasion when I was about ten years old. A group of us children were collecting our diminutive catch. I slipped on a rock and fell backwards into the stream. The water was cold after a heavy night's rain. The ground was wet and slippery. My feet went from under me and down I fell on my backside into the stream. What a shock I got as the cold water swirled around my waist. I was hastily pulled from the stream by my accomplices and an emergency conference held as we stood at the edge of the road. They decided that there was nothing for it but to bring me into Bolands' and dry me by the fire that the occupants kept burning both summer and winter.

Mr and Mrs Boland were an elderly couple who lived about three-quarters of a mile from us. A veteran of both the Boer and the 1914-18 War, Mr Boland worked as a gardener at our house. The couple had ten children, the youngest two of whom were about our age. Visiting Bolands' was something we were not supposed to do. Mrs Boland insisted on serving up large helpings of fresh loaf bread and jam. Visits were strictly forbidden by my mother, as she felt it was, as she put it, "taking food out of the mouths of the poor."

This was hard for us to comprehend since, the woman we called, "Mrs Joe" always had plenty of fresh loaf cut and spread with shop jam whenever we happened to call. This day was no different. The bread was already heaped with jam and stacked on a large plate on the table, as if Mrs Joe knew that one of us might have an accident.

There was six of us children altogether in the kitchen – myself, my younger sister and brother, plus three cousins from Dublin. Five of us were about to make a beeline for the heaped plate of bread and jam. We were, however, stopped in our tracks when my younger brother, as was his wont, took charge. He reminded everyone that there was one well-soaked elder brother and a pair of dripping trousers to be seen to first.

We had an emergency on our hands – there could be no doubt about that as I stood there, water dripping from my trousers onto the stone flags of the kitchen floor. There was, however, an obvious solution to the problem. At the end of the room was a blazing fire. Even in midsummer, the fire blazed brightly in the open grate. For one, it was the only means of cooking to be had. This was of course before rural electrification.

I was led by my brother and Mrs Joe as near to the fire as was safe, without running the risk of my clothes being scorched. Having delivered me to the fire, my brother retreated to the table laden with bread and jam. Mrs Joe settled into an armchair at the other side of the open fire. It blazed so brightly and fiercely, I could feel the fingers of heat begin to permeate my cold damp trousers, from which steam started to rise. Within half an hour or so, my trousers and limbs had dried out. The feast of bread and jam could now begin for me.

Everyone was now relaxed. There would be no need for Annabelle – or Hannabelle, as she would later be christened – to ever find out. My mother acquired this nickname after my brother and I had entered secondary education and learned the lines of a famous Yankee poem, *Barbara Frietchie* by John Greenleaf Whittier, some of which, I think, went like this:

Save your country's flag cries she
When Lee marched over the mountain wall...

My brother altered this to:

When Lee comes over the garden wall...

Irrespective of what we called our mother, we were adamant that she would never know that I had had such an accident at the stream – or river, as it seemed to us. We knew that our maid, Teresa, would never tell. Mrs Joe would warn her husband, Boland that he was not to mention it either, especially not at Doonvarna, the house in which we lived.

Father

One of the most laborious tasks my father had to undertake was to enter, in his official ledgers and receipt books, details of funds dispersed, as well as a record of every person, item and job involved. All this was done in three different colours – blue, red and green. I well recall the ink-stained table-cloth that covered the dining-room table as my father sat down to officially record the functions he performed as Home Assistance Officer, which replaced the old position of Relieving Officer under the Poor Law. Not only had this been a very bureaucratic system, it had been a harsh one, inasmuch as the strict means test had, in most cases, placed the recipient on an obligatory footing. The new system was much less rigid; the Home Assistance Officers had more discretion when it came to the disbursal of funds. All the Officer had to do was satisfy himself that the individual was in need. Although only a small improvement, this advance was as much as the new State could manage, given the economic circumstances of the time. The change from

Relieving Officers to Home Assistance Officers was viewed, nevertheless, as a whole new departure: the least that could be expected from our own new native administration.

Another of the Welfare programmes was one for boarded-out children. It was concerned with finding homes – other than orphanages and other such institutions – for orphaned or neglected children. It was, in fact, a form of fostering. The children were placed with suitable families – in most cases, poor families.

The implementation of these programmes was at the discretion of the Local Authority. Their supervision was left very much in the hands of the Home Assistance Officer. This had repercussions for the Officer and his family, as needy people who lived locally could turn up any time day or night, though mostly in the evenings. My father would interview such people on the doorstep. If he considered their claims justified he would issue them with financial assistance or food vouchers, though mostly vouchers. If someone called who was definitely in need but, for some reason or other did not fulfil the necessary requirements, he would dip into his own pocket and give them a handout. This, my mother disapproved of because she was from a different background – a "business background", in her own words. Before marrying, she had served her time to business and she didn't like the idea of handouts on her own doorstep.

Another of my father's duties was to visit all the dispensaries in the area, which in this case stretched as far as Ardee. There must have been ten dispensaries in all. Most of the administration of the new Welfare System was carried out from a room in the Officer's own house, or from the local dispensary. Each dispensary had a doctor from whom, the poor who could not afford a family doctor, could seek medical assistance. To avail of this however, they had to present themselves on certain designated days.

The country then was poor and largely dependent on agriculture. There was very little manufacturing. Work in the agricultural sector was of a purely seasonal nature, leaving only the County Councils to provide labouring jobs, mostly making roads. Although this was not a pensionable occupation, it was, nonetheless, a position sought after by most labouring men. The Free State Government set about erecting high tariff walls in order to foster manufacturing, which had been set up to supply local needs and to help alleviate the need for social welfare. The need for exports was met by the transport of cattle, mostly on the hoof. This was the way until the 1970s, when the government decided, and the general population concurred – that it would be better to slaughter cattle in this country in order to provide added value and secure employment. This Welfare and other social improvements cost money.

The relationship between Church and State remained especially close. It was not unusual for prominent politicians to declare that they were Catholics first, Irishmen second and politicians third.

Chapter Two:
My Childhood

I was born into this world on 23 May 1939. It was a difficult birth and the prognosis was not good, for I had cerebral palsy, otherwise known as 'an accident of birth'. The only hope that the doctor could offer to my mother was that a suitable residential institution could be found, that would care for me for the rest of my life, one that might be long or mercifully short. This, the doctor pronounced in the suitably authoritative voice of an eminent medical man.

"This child," he said, "will be unlikely ever to walk – or even talk – in any meaningful or coherent way."

He felt it essential that a suitable institution would be found with all possible haste, so that the unfortunate child could be placed in the hands of experts: those with either the necessary training – or a strong religious vocation– to look after the sick and indigent.

My mother, however, was intent on ignoring this negative advice, so willingly and dogmatically offered by the good doctor. As a businesswoman, she knew that where there was a will, there was a way. So began, for my mother and I, the innumerable calls on the great and the good in medical circles. Some of these – Sir Arthur Chance, for example – were highly qualified. Others were much less qualified; some even had qualifications of very suspicious provenance.

But my mother was desperate, determined to try anything, regardless of what it cost financially and time wise.

Doctors said that my mother's dream of my living a normal and fulfilled life could never be achieved. They were the experts and had seen many times, the heart-breaking consequences of unfulfilled promises of healing. There were those of another view however, notably a young doctor named Robert Collis, who had become something of an expert on cerebral palsy. He had a number of clinics scattered around Dublin city, staffed by young idealistic medicos. He believed that people like me could be helped to lead a relatively normal life. I never actually met the good Dr Collis himself, though I did attend one of his cerebral palsy clinics from time to time.

One, I distinctly remember, was in Clontarf, another in Islandbridge, where I believe we may have got a close up view of the late Christy Brown. This was around the time of the publication of *My Left Foot*, serialized in the *Evening Herald*. To the general public, Christy's achievements were a remarkable example of physical and mental compensation. To this day, his achievement is held in enormous regard. To the medical and educational establishment however, it bordered on folly. This was, after all, a time when anyone who wrote with their left hand was considered almost demonic: someone to be ridiculed and abused. There was a word in Irish for such people: *Ciotóg* and such people were regarded with the greatest of suspicion.

I recall these visits to Dublin to consult with a prominent medical man, who would instruct my mother on how to try out some new regime of exercise. I even remember us calling on one highly recommended quack. But mostly, these trips were for the purpose of validating the various physiotherapy regimes administered to me by my mother, with the assistance of the local Jubilee nurse. We would leave Kells in the early hours of the morning, by the first train of the day, when the morning dew still sparkled on the spring and summer bedding in the half-moon flowerbeds, placed at intervals along the lower wall of the station. Such an early start would allow my mother to do some shopping in the city centre, before travelling to my Aunt Chrissie's house in Rathfarnham.

In the late 40s and early 50s, there was an institution in that suburb – one of which Doctor Collis spoke – which looked after people with a disability. As far as I can remember, disabled people were drawn around in bathchairs – the wheelchairs of the 18-19th centuries. This mode of transport involved the disabled person being pulled along by a fit male attendant. Walking some distance behind these bathchairs – usually in pairs – were sisters of a religious congregation that was in charge of particular institutions that cared for these 'unfortunate invalids' or 'cripples', as we were called at the time.

These were the Little Sisters of the Assumption or – as they were known locally – the French Nuns. They wore habits of blue and white aprons and high-winged headdresses, or 'wimples'. This was the typical dress of the French peasant woman of the 16-17th centuries. They seemed so numerous that one could be forgiven for thinking that the greater portion of the population of Dublin – and more especially Rathfarnham – was composed of French Nuns and invalid carriage attendants, with most of the remainder being disabled people in bathchairs. It looked like something out of the grotto at Lourdes.

We would make our way through the streets of suburban Dublin with as much haste as we could muster. This was not very fast as I was a very slow walker and very unsteady on my feet. By the time we reached the residence of the Murray family, my Aunt Chrissie would have a meal prepared. After we had finished the meal, I and the other children would be ushered through the French windows into the garden. It was thought important that I get as much fresh air and exercise as possible if I were to grow up strong and healthy.

Out on the back lawn, my cousins, who attended Terenure College, had set up a wicket for a game of cricket. Cousin Tommy would elect to defend the wicket while his brother, Oliver, would bowl the first over. As it was at play, so it was in their other lives, for Tommy was forever defending. He was always supportive and concerned for other people's needs. Oliver, on the other hand, was always challenging. The relationship between these two brothers mirrored, to some extent, that between myself and my brother, John. I was more passive and John was more adventurous. It could also be described as having just a small element of competition.

Tommy had a natural grace and dexterity, which people found engaging. He had taught himself conjuring tricks and could produce pennies – even shillings – from behind the flowering head of a Scotch thistle or a stately Russell lupin: a skill that intrigued us all. This was white magic at its finest. He was also a very fine draughtsman; his drawings being largely derived from popular comics of the day.

The attraction of sports such as cricket and tennis is, for me, enhanced by the associated glorious nostalgia. During the summer ritual of after-tea cricket, I would be seated in a deckchair, watching the others perform their slow ritual dance of bowling and batting. It now seems strange but always, when I think of a game of cricket, the images that spring to mind all play out in slow motion. But then, this is a strange game: more of an art than a sport. It is a game in which the ambience becomes part of the game itself. The ritual: a sound of willow against leather followed by slow, sporadic bursts of applause whenever a successful run has been completed.

There is nothing to compare with cricket in loveliness except a good game of tennis. With tennis, there is the sound of ball against strings and the suggestive call of the umpire: Love 15, advantage Miss Wade … reminiscent of long-legged girls such as the Miss Joan Hunter Dunn of John Betjeman fame. Tennis, too, left its impression upon me, though once again, I was destined to be a spectator, whether it was at the hard court at Skerries or the smaller hard court at the rear of the St Vincent de Paul Hall in Kells. The lawn tennis court that had shared a boundary with our garden at home was, by this time, no more, having reverted to a meadow.

The Clinic

On the appointed day, my mother and I would set out in the morning for the clinic of the designated expert. Aunt Chrissie would, oft-times, accompany us. The two sisters would each take hold of one of my hands, so that I could swing between them as if I were an actual swing. This would further embellish my exercise regime, for it reinforced the muscles in my upper body and arms – and was in line with medical advice. Carrying me in their arms or a buggy (or go-kart as it was known at the time) was strictly forbidden by the experts. Although I did not appreciate it at the time, this was the best advice that any medical practitioner could have given. Thinking back on it now, the suggestions for such exercises came from my mother and her sisters – but mostly from my mother, for she was a practical woman who could readily appreciate the value of physical activity.

One of the doctors whom we attended was a Mr Lane, who lived in a large Victorian terraced house, situated on a tree-lined drive that led from one side of the Smithfield cattle mart down to the rear of the Phoenix Park. In spring and summer, these trees cast dappled shadows on the pavement which, on very hot days, rendered the whole avenue both cool and comfortable. In autumn and winter, the broad leaves fell from this canopy to lie in fiery drifts along the inner pathways, ledges and railings in front of the terraced houses. When we reached Mr Lane's house, we ascended the flight of granite steps leading up to his front door. Since first coming to Mr Lane's clinic, my walking and general mobility had improved. I was now more steady on my feet and could mount these steps. In fact, I was determined to be allowed to surmount those last obstacles to freedom, with as little assistance as possible from the two women who usually accompanied me.

Mr Lane was a friendly man: a bachelor who lived with his widowed mother in this rather large, Victorian terraced house with a redbrick exterior and a huge front garden. I was already familiar with the interior of establishments such as these. On our many trips to Dublin – but especially on occasions when the Murray family were away – my mother and I would stay with my father's sister (Aunt Katie) who lived in just such a house in Glasnevin, in a street just off Botanic Avenue. I can vividly recall the interior of that house. As I stood at the bottom of the interior stairway, I could see the steps ascending to floor after floor.

Although Mr Lane was a quiet and gentle man, his mother was the exact opposite – a house-proud, domineering woman who took it for granted that all those entering her front door were bound by her inflexible house rules. Hence the various nicknames that aunts and nannies and their charges gave her. The sobriquet 'Sergeant Major' was one that quite suited. I would, one day, come into conflict with this formidable woman with the fearsome reputation.

It was inconceivable that my mother, or any other woman present would be allowed exchange words with the 'Sergeant Major'. On this particular occasion the traffic through the waiting room to Mr. Lane's clinic flowed smoothly and briskly. While my mother and I waited our turn, I made my way over to the window, to look out on the street. To do this, I had to pass two lengthy laced curtains that hung from the pediment down to the floor.

Outside, the sun cast dappled shadows on the roadway, on the pavement and the half of the garden that lay nearest the road. A typical late spring scene. All was peaceful. The room was filled with women's chatter.

In order to peer out the window, I had parted company temporarily with my mother. All of a sudden, a young woman's voice rose above the general hum and chatter, "Oh, the child! The Sergeant Major ...."

The young woman swooped down and swept me into her arms, kissing me on the forehead. She was one of the women who regularly attended the consulting rooms, along with her daughter. I didn't know who she was but she smelt sweet and fragrant.

"Darling," she whispered glancing out the window towards the road, "the Sergeant Major!"

I followed her glance but saw nothing suspicious, nothing to be alarmed about, only an elderly woman coming through the entrance gate. This woman was dowdily dressed in an old-fashioned kind of way.

The young woman tightened her embrace and whispered "darling" once more, as she swept me past my mother and the other women and children in the waiting room. All eyes were focussed, not on the young woman but on the heavy door with its light green ceramic knob. Again, she kissed me and brushed my burning cheeks with her own cool cheeks and soft lips. "I think I will keep you," she said in a loud whisper intended to be heard by all in the room.

She continued the sweep towards her own chair with me in her arms. Before seating herself, she smiled and gestured towards my mother who returned a knowing smile. I could feel the woman's heart throbbing beneath her light summer dress. I hoped this excited throbbing was for me and not occasioned by some vague foreboding of what was surely to come. Her smile was meant to reassure me that she was my protector. The apprehension in the other women however was palpable. Still clasping me to her bosom the young woman in rapid succession cast fearful glances to that heavy brown door with its green ceramic knob.

Suddenly the knob turned, the door opened, and there stood a seemingly frail old woman poised threateningly. The frailty rapidly dissolved to reveal a forbidding, even threatening figure. She glanced menacingly about the room. All the women, except for my mother and my protector, seemed to draw back, cowering beneath the withering formidable stare.

"What was that child doing at my window?" she demanded, pointing an accusing finger at me.

My protector drew breath as I buried my face in her comforting bosom. "He was merely inquisitive. Is there anything so terribly wrong in that?" she replied in a defiant tone, with a lioness's growl of protection.

So clear was the message and the intent that the Sergeant Major took a step backwards. Emboldened by this slight hesitation, the young woman took a step forward towards her adversary.

"What was that child doing behind my lace curtains?" cried the Sergeant Major, once again pointing an accusing finger at me.

My protector continued to press me to her breast. Once more, I could feel the heartbeats beneath her light summer dress.

"Ssh!" she whispered down to me, "Ssh, my little sweetheart." Again, she kissed me on my forehead and lips. "He is only a child. What wrong has he done anyway, only looking onto the public roadway?"

The older woman threw a quick furtive glance over her shoulder, as if looking for an escape route, then turned to face down the young challenger. She stood her ground and hissed: "I shall remind you that it is my window – and my curtains!"

The young woman replied defiantly, "And I shall remind you that this is a public waiting-room."

Sensing that she was on the brink of an ignominious defeat, the older woman again hissed, "We shall have to see about that, Madam!"

Turning, she marched through the door, heading out to the entrance hall from whence she came. Everyone waited in fearful silence, afraid that she might knock on the door to the room where Mr Lane was in consultation. That is exactly what she did. All the women strained to hear what was being said but could catch nothing but whispers. After a short time, the Sergeant Major retreated up the corridor. We could then hear doors in the living quarters overhead being slammed.

There followed an uneasy silence, broken only by sporadic outbursts of light coughing and edgy frightened sobs from the children. All the mothers and nannies had lifted their young charges onto their knees for safety's sake. That is, all except for my mother and the young woman who held me in her arms as she sat defiantly on her chair. She intoned again in a whisper, "Ssh! My little sweetheart," rocking me in her arms.

A wood-panelled partition divided Mr Lane's consulting room from the waiting room in which we sat. Suddenly, one section of the partition opened slowly and hesitantly. Mr Lane stepped into the waiting room. He had a broad beaming smile on his face. The women could clearly see that that man was not the same shy diffident fellow they had known in the years attending the clinic. He was now a happy, confident and – in a curious kind of way – handsome young man.

"Well ladies, is everything all right?" he enquired in a most pleasant tone.

"Everything is just hunky dory," one women volunteered. The rest intoned murmurs of agreement.

"Good, good." he replied, "Hunky dory! That's what I like to hear."

Then, turning to my protector, who had, by now, returned me to my mother, he beckoned her to follow him into his consulting room. With a smile on her lips and holding the hand of her own young daughter, the woman followed Mr Lane. As she passed by, the other women gave her a round of applause. I was thrilled with the response.

The next morning, we would all be returning to Kells, where my father would be brought up to speed on my progress. Little did I know that his calming presence would not be around to sustain us in the years ahead.

In fact, my father never came with us to Dublin. He left the negotiations with medical men in the hands of my mother, who had the dominant role in our household. My father was, however, always referred to as "the boss". Whenever the door was opened to a countryman tugging his forelock and enquiring, "G'day Mam, is the boss at home?" it was enough to raise my mother's ire. She felt strongly that she should make all the major decisions. Nevertheless, out of propriety, she kept a respectful silence.

My father was a tall handsome man of placid demeanour. My mother, on the other hand, was fiery and, like most of her sisters, opinionated. Through medical neglect, my father, however would soon be dead – and at a very early age. At that time, paper clips were rarely used and staples virtually unknown. Forms and documents were fastened together with pins. Unfortunately, my father left some of these pins in a coat pocket and forgot about them. They rusted. He scratched himself and got blood poisoning. The wounds festered causing severe poisoning in the hand and up the arm.

To add to our troubles, the family doctor was an old man whose advice was to apply a bread poultice. Eventually the poisoning got so bad my father was brought to his bed. But within a day, he was dying. The poisoning had spread to the brain. I remember my brother, John, being called to fetch the doctor, who was just in time to witness my father's last breath and pronounce him dead. He was only 57. I was seven years old at the time. I couldn't bring myself to go in and see his body. My brother and sister did, however. I feared that we would be put in an orphanage but my mother quickly quelled that fear. All the same, life thereafter would be changed utterly.

Neighbours and Servants

Now that my mother had been satisfied that my exercise regime was firmly in place, it was time to consider my formal education, which was, at the time – as it still is – considered to be the very foundation of a child's school career. My younger brother, John, had started in what was popularly known as babies' class, in the Convent of Mercy at the far end of town. He left the house every morning and returned at two every afternoon. He was brought there by Bolands' second-youngest daughter, Teresa, who, it was always considered, would make a very suitable housemaid in place of her elder sister, Eileen, whenever she got married – and whenever the nuns decided that Teresa had received as much education as her simple mind could absorb. The departure from the classroom would be sooner rather than later, due to what the nuns described as her slow-wittedness. Teresa was steeped in country lore and her reply to most questions of any substance was, "The best goods come in small parcels". This was taken to be a reference to her own slight stature.

Those quaint sayings mystified us, as they did our parents. As comments, they were descriptive but little more. As statements, they held no commandments and gave no orders or even instructions. Teresa was also a devout believer in fairies – of whom she was suspicious – and in ghosts and ghouls – of which she was definitely afraid.

Sometimes, we would cover ourselves in white sheets and wait for Teresa to emerge from the house on her way home. This was a game for us, reserved especially for late autumn and early winter, when the first frosts had barely touched the leaves and flower heads. The trees in Carolans' fields were already in their full autumn colours, as were the trees in the other fields that bordered our garden. We would jump out from behind the herbaceous borders with the sheets draped over our shoulders. Poor Teresa would utter a frightened scream, crying as she ran out the gate and down the road, "Jesus, Mary and Joseph, save us from all harm!"

To our childish minds, this was a spot of fun, something to liven up the long winters' nights but for Teresa, it was a frightening experience. For that reason, I now regret those childish games, as I recall them, for what they were.

Teresa was unlike her sisters: she was shy and timid by nature and would remain so for the rest of her life. She lived in a closed world. In short, a world of what she called "the pictures". Most of her retorts were taken directly from either local folklore or whatever was currently on show at the local cinema. I can well remember some of the expressions with which she met the world and defended herself. One such saying was "gone with the wind", used when she wished to convey that something local was missing. If someone behaved in what she regarded as a foolish fashion, she would say that they were acting just like "the three stooges".

Books and Radio

One of my many sources of education was the radio. Due to my cerebral palsy, I was unable to sustain prolonged periods of even moderately active play. My mother had always insisted that I should, for the sake of good muscle development, take part in as much activity as possible. But if the games became too strenuous, I could withdraw to the safety of the large armchair by the radio and read a book – or perhaps listen to the radio itself.

In our house, as elsewhere in rural Ireland, the News and Weather were very important. Every day, the radio was turned on without fail, for the Evening News at 6pm so that the happenings of the world could be heard and judged. The radio was then left on while everyone went about their business, so that eventually we would hear the 9pm News and any changes that had occurred in the intervening three hours. These were rare in those days, when the world seemed to spin more slowly on its axis.

Radio Éireann would begin broadcasting at 8am each day and continue until after the main News was broadcast at 9am. The station then closed down until 12 noon. News and Weather reports were vital for the rural populace, as they no doubt were for the nation as a whole. Above all, it was vital to the farming community to have an accurate knowledge of the weather they were likely to encounter during the day. To this end, in our household, the forecast could be either confirmed or denied by what was commonly referred to as 'the glass', but was more scientifically known as a barometer.

My father would give the instrument a couple of sharp light raps with his knuckles, which would tell whether the glass was "up" or "down", to use the expressions of the time. If the little arrows on the dial swung towards dry or fine, the glass was said to be "up"; towards wet or stormy it was said to be "down". Callers to the door constantly asked my father if he could tell them whether the glass was "up" or down". My father would consult the barometer and pronounce the verdict, thus confirming or denying the radio forecast. Mostly the two were in very near agreement. Occasionally there were very sharp divisions between the two forecasts. This was, for me, an education – albeit an informal one – on the uses and challenges of new technology, which became all the more demanding as time passed and the world accelerated on its axis.

Chapter Three:
My Education

Leaving informal education aside, my formal education had begun. There were, however, two problems. One was that my eyesight was not all that good, although this was not recognised until I was in first class at the local CBS National School. As well as my poor eyesight, my handwriting was completely illegible. It was decided that I would have private tuition. To this end a lady, Mrs Coyne, was hired to give me private lessons.

Mrs Coyne was a very kind and generous woman, a retired National School teacher who lived with her husband in a row of four houses, owned by my uncle, Dennis, on the main Kells-Trim road, locally known as the Gardenrath Road. Gardenrath was the name of the townland through which this road ran, extending from the south-eastern boundary of the town, out as far as the cottages inhabited by a Mr and Mrs Mooney and the Caffrey family.

My mother warned me not to stare at Mrs Coyne's face, as it might cause offence, due to the fact that her nose was disfigured. Local lore had it that when she was a newly wedded bride, she had been preparing her husband's breakfast. There was a splattering in the frying pan and a piece of very hot grease flew up and caught the unfortunate woman on the nose. It left an indelible mark for the rest of her life.

I recall many incidents from my very earliest school life as if they happened only yesterday and experience again the moods that they engendered. The earliest such experience was of the National School located at the end of the monastery yard in Bective Street. The long school building had three entrances. Through the south porch, one entered the Second and Third classrooms. Through the centre porch, one entered the First and Fourth classrooms. Through the north porch, one entered the Fifth and Sixth classrooms, where the big boys were. They were a formidable group, as they were much taller than me and wore long trousers that tended to emphasise their manliness. This was as it should be since most of the Sixth Class would – having reached the ripe old age of fourteen – be moving on to their first year at the Secondary School, which was located at the top of the yard, through an arch beyond the handball alley. During designated periods, the entire Primary school would be out at play. There could be anything up to two hundred boys, of all sizes and levels of physical fitness, milling about the yard.

I had to be very careful lest I be knocked down and hurt – even seriously injured – by a player in one of the many games that crisscrossed the big yard. All of this went to feed my feelings of being different. Those feelings of insecurity were occasionally intensified when I caught a glimpse of my teacher staring down from the high windows that overlooked the yard. Eventually however – and happily for me – a bell would be rung by a slender figure in a black cassock. One of the brothers. This was the bell that summoned the scholars from play to study.

Inside the classroom, Brother Hinchy would continue the lesson that had been broken off for play. He would complete his maths lessons as quickly as he could before telling us to put away our books. This we did with the utmost speed, for we knew that he was going to tell us a story. The elderly and kindly brother was a consummate storyteller. His subject was normally Cuchulainn or Cormac MacAirt. On the occasions when he told the story of MacAirt, he began by quoting the lines of Samuel Ferguson:

But bury me at Rossnaree
And face me to the rising sun

The whole class was enthralled. But for me there was a particular sadness to these occasions. I would have to leave at least an hour early, to continue my lessons with Mrs Coyne at her home.

Before I leave the subject of school, I must say something about the décor of this particular institution, notably the arrangement of the First Class room. The room was unusual in that, along the back wall hung ten miniature-size Edwardian prints of beach scenes with old-fashioned bathing machines. None of the beaches with which we had been acquainted as children – on summer trips to Mornington, Laytown or Bettystown – were like this. Although the prints were incongruous with the setting, they did have a certain charm. No doubt, they were presented to the school by some local worthy, the Taylors of Headfort House most likely. In the centre of the outer wall, facing towards a field known as The Bottoms, was a large open fireplace. In winter, this was a most sought after place in which to occupy a desk.

As Brother Hinchy warmed to the theme of his story, a hush descended on the class. Every boy, without exception, was drawn into these heroic tales of courage. He regaled the class for about three quarters of an hour. Then, he would stop abruptly and glance up at the clock that hung high on the wall above the framed prints. He would then glance down at me to indicate that it was time I was gone. With reluctance, I gathered up my schoolbooks and made my departure for Mrs Coyne's. As I pulled the classroom door behind me, Brother Hinchy's mellifluous tones quickly regained the attention of his hushed audience of the boys of the First Class. He really warmed to his subject as he continued to relate his marvellous tales.

What sadness and loss I felt as I walked up the forlorn and deserted yard, Brother Hinchy's voice receding in the distance! This sadness did not a lift until I reached Mrs Coyne's front door. As I slowly ascended the stone steps leading to the hall door, I began to think of the cupcakes that would be served with our tea break. Indeed, this partly compensated for missing the ending of Brother Hinchy's tale of heroism.

The inside of Mrs Coyne's house was like no other. The entrance hall was the first surprise of this seemingly modest suburban villa. It was filled on every side with potted ferns, planted in Victorian delph flowerpots. But the floral designs were obscured by the lush, even rampant, vegetation that imbued the hallway with a cavernous aspect, as if it were some kind of a fairy grotto. At least that was the impression it left on me. Others might disagree, preferring to describe the potted ferns as weeds. Some might even be horrified, thinking that the wilderness had broken into the Coyne household. These ferns were not of the cultivated variety but were wild ones, which grew in profusion in drains, ditches and boggy areas in the locality. Even the back drawing room, which looked out onto the Coyne's long back lawn and orchard, contained potted ferns dispersed at intervals around the room and on the upright piano that stood against the wall. There was even one large specimen placed on the table where I studied my reading and writing, under the kind and benevolent gaze of Mrs Coyne.

Did she ever allude to the dense foliage of the elvan grove in which she lived with her husband? Yes, she did. This diminutive lady, all dressed in black silk and white lace would draw my attention to some seasonable changes, observing the ever-thickening vegetation that slowly but surely crept across the floor of the hallway, into every nook and cranny, threatening to turn her semi-detached suburban house into a fairy dell. As she poured me a cup of tea, or held out a plate full of cupcakes, she would, with a wondrous sweep of the other arm, indicate the ferns. She would ask whether I had noticed any change in the collection.

"No, not since yesterday," I would reply.

"No, no my dear. Since last week!"

"Yes," I would reply, "they have grown."

Mrs Coyne held me in a fixed and questioning stare, "Since last month, my dear?"

"A little," I offered in reply, for I knew just where this was heading.

"Since last summer?" she asked.

"A lot," I replied briskly, anxious to get to the point of our little chat.

A moment's silence.

"And ...?" Mrs Coyne enquired, her stare intensifying still more.

I glanced over her shoulder at the large flowerpot on the table. Clearly, the plant was sprouting juvenile foliage from the base of the old leaves. This new growth was covered in soft, downy, brown fur, which I pointed out to her.

"Ha!" Mrs Coyne exclaimed, as she lay back in her chair holding a cup and saucer. Oh! How I wished that I could hold a cup and saucer with such ease and grace! But no, I had to cup both hands around my mug and lift it slowly to my lips.

Mrs Coyne continued to study me as I watched. "Ah, yes!" she said after an interval, her voice soft and low, almost reverent, "The miracle of nature."

And so she went on for some time, until she eventually raised the subject of my future. "When the time comes would you like to go to Warrenstown College to study horticulture?" she enquired.

She was the first person I ever heard use this word, 'horticulture'. It seemed very big at the time – it certainly was not in any of the books we were reading. But, as she explained to me, horticulture was about the science of growing things. She liked growing wild ferns in as many varieties as she and her husband could find in the locality. I liked more exotic cultivars, however. In a sheltered corner of the garden at home, I had made what I regarded as a mini-glasshouse out of two pieces of discarded broken window-glass, by leaning them one against the other. Here I sowed some pips from oranges and grapefruit, also the seeds of apples.

Under Mrs Coyne's tutelage, my reading and arithmetic progressed enormously. My handwriting however, remained the problem, not through any lack of intellectual ability on my part and certainly not on the part of Mrs Coyne. No, the problem was a physical one that stemmed from my cerebral palsy. This inability to write legibly remains with me to this day.

Mrs Coyne taught me many coping skills, principal amongst them the development of memory. I could memorise a lot of information, storing it in my mind until I could use what is commonly referred to, in computer speak, as downloading. This meant finding someone with a more legible hand than my own. Not that there were not plenty of people with flawless handwriting. It seemed that everyone else's handwriting was more legible my own.

The task of helping me download this information required an accomplice who needed my skills with language. Invariably, the task fell to my younger sister, who also needed help with school essays (or compositions, as they were known). Superficially, this seemed an ideal solution but there were certain inherent tensions stemming from the fact that I had developed an abiding love of the English language and delighted in what were called 'big' words – words such as horticulture or catharsis or apotheosis – which I always looked for an opportunity to use in my notes, or in my sister's compositions. This made my sister's teachers suspicious, as they began to suspect that my sister did not write the piece herself. How could a 12-year-old girl know and understand such words?

The nuns considered themselves experts in what girls of any age were interested in. It certainly was not big words. This forced me to reconsider– albeit reluctantly– such words and the use to which they could be put. They obviously could not be used in my sister's essays. I got it hard to confine the use of such words to note taking only. That I was able to restrain myself to do so I ascribe to two things: first, I had learned a method of reining in my enthusiasm; secondly, that my sister would immediately spell the word. Usually I got it right but, on the occasions when I gave the wrong spelling, she instantly held it up as a reason why I should use a smaller word.

Mrs Coyne also provided me with a method of note taking. It was simplicity itself. It was based on the fact that my handwriting was illegible to anyone but me. The suggestion was this: why not put points down on paper and expand them further when called on to do so by my sister? Since these prompts were legible to me, it worked spectacularly well, especially when it came to the dictation of essays for my sister.

The fact that Mrs Coyne could invent coping skills to enable me to master some seemingly insurmountable problems, meant that she was a mentor far ahead of her time. Nowadays, her skills would be in great demand. Also, like my mother and her sisters, she was a very practical woman in spite of the fairy dell in which she and her husband lived. I shall always be grateful to her for teaching me the difference between appearance and reality. This would stand me in good stead throughout my academic career.

Every evening, after I had completed my studies with Mrs Coyne, I would return to my home and set myself down by the radio for a couple of enrapt hours, listening, it must be said to the BBC Home Service. This was the beginning of a second but very significant strand of my education. Although I did not know it at the time, I was being introduced to the glories of American, European and Russian literature. This was a strange world of sad and despairing people being turned out of their orchards, never again to contemplate the annual blossom of the cherry tree and the equally miraculous ripening of the red berries. It reminded me of that Garden of Eden which our ancestors had lost.

Chapter Four:
Early Adulthood – Discovering Literature

Most days my mother took an afternoon nap for an hour or two. However, two days a week she would go into town to do her shopping. On those days, our housemaid, Teresa, would be under strict instructions to clean all the floors and rooms in the house. She would start by washing and mopping the tiled floor in the kitchen and scullery (or pantry, as she would have it). The hallway had to be hoovered, also the dining room and drawing room, before starting on the stairs. Then she would tackle the entire upstairs.

It always annoyed me that she would wring out the wet floor cloth just as I seated myself in the big armchair to listen to the radio. When she switched on the vacuum cleaner, to hoover the staircase and top stair bedrooms, the radio picked up all the interference generated by the hoover. It became impossible to hear anything except for the crackle of static. This used to so infuriate me that I would unplug the infernal machine at the socket. This left poor Teresa halfway up the stairs wondering what had happened. After I had done this on a couple of occasions, I was given a good talking to by my mother and reminded that nothing should interfere with the smooth running of her household.

Despite the disruption caused by the infernal vacuum cleaner, I was, however, able to experience the great dramatists of the late 19th and early 20th century – Ibsen, Chekhov, Miller and O'Neill amongst others. I also experienced the great classic novelists of the English language – Dickens and Stevenson for example. I heard *Oliver Twist* and *Kidnapped* read over the radio: but it was the dramatists and their works which made the greatest impression upon me.

On hearing a single speech, even if I could not recognise the play from which it came I could at least identify its author. In the meantime, my cousins, the Murrays, had become avid readers and had built up an impressive collection of paperbacks, mostly Penguin classics.

The 1950s and 60s saw a revolution in paperback publishing of what were then called modern classics – and of contemporary books. These could be purchased for as little as five shillings. Slender volumes could be had for as little as 2/6.

When I visited my cousins – who were now living in Skerries – for my summer holidays, my days were filled with literature. All the great works of the World were at my fingertips. I have a vivid memory of sitting on a bench on the rocky promontory, just before Red Island Holiday Camp, reading the latest edition of Chekhov's short stories. How I wished I could emulate him. But the eternal problem remained: to find a way of transforming my thoughts into some sort of legible writing.

Early Writing

My ever patient sister and I had an unwritten agreement that she would transcribe my thoughts in exchange for help with her school compositions: but she wisely put an embargo on what she termed "fancy" words or phrases. This, I felt, rather cramped my style – until my mother's elder sister (Aunt Mary) took the matter in hand and bought me a second-hand typewriter, an old-fashioned Underwood. It was the kind of instrument you had to pound very hard to make the right impression on the page. This made the whole process slow and laborious.

I did, however, manage to hammer out a short story of about 2,500 words, entitled *The Sight of the Blind*. It was my interpretation of how a sightless person built up a picture of nature and of the world around him. It was a piece of juvenilia, as I now realise, but to me, with that peculiar innocence of the novice scribe, it would have had pieces of pure genius embedded therein. One of my other cousins, Noel Martin, who lived in a big house in Glasnevin, offered to show the story to a friend of his who worked as an editor with the publishing house, Browne and Nolan, which operated out of an office and shop in Nassau Street.

So, with the help of my mother and sister, I sent off my manuscript to the publishers and awaited a reply with equal amounts of both anticipation and trepidation. Anticipation, because I felt justified in the belief that the editor would surely spot the signs of genius embedded in the text. Trepidation, since I was fearful that he would find it dull and uninteresting, with precious little to say and that he would miss the efforts I had made to create atmosphere.

In due course, a letter arrived complimenting me on the plot and for having created a complete story. He felt however, that I needed to pay more attention to syntax. He also provided a reading list, which included writers such as

Chekhov, Turgenev and Seán O Faoláin. He recommended Frank O'Connor's *Guests of the Nation* and Hemingway's collection of short stories, *Men Without Women*.

Although unfamiliar with those writers, my eye settled on the last two mentioned. I tossed it over in my mind: "Would I read O'Connor or would I read Hemingway?"

I eventually settled on Hemingway's *Men Without Women*, my first introduction to that author and his short staccato sentences. In a way, I found his writing strangely evocative and replete with atmosphere – though not of the gloomy Russian type. The atmosphere he created was heavy with the dust and sun of southern Spain and the green wilderness of North American lakes and rivers, in which his heroes hunted and fished. He portrayed the world of masculine sportsmen who lived in a world deprived of femininity. Hence his title, *Men Without Women*. It included a story about boxing, involving individuals in the solitary pursuit of their personal goals. As for fishing, this was, in Hemingway's days at least, a solitary pursuit which women would have found hard to understand.

My reading of the great writers enabled me to examine both the methods whereby they unfolded their narratives and the stories that lay behind all of life. Little did I know it then but this would coincide with the advice I was given many years later, by that grand old dame of letters, Mary Lavin: to the effect that I should read not just for pleasure but also, to dissect and question the methods employed, as a student should. This was sound advice coming from Mary, who was herself a recognised mistress of the short story form. Applying this method, I would find myself reading a passage of Hemingway over and over again, just to hear how he handled the situation in prose. I learnt the crucial lesson that it is often more important to hint at something, to suggest rather than to state emphatically that such and such was the case.

At this time, the essential faculties of mind and spirit were developing within me. This included the faculty of the imagination, something not much praised in the Ireland of the 1950s. In fact, it was actually despised by many people, who shared with Mr Squeers (a character in Dickens' novel, *Nicholas Nickleby*) the belief that a sound education ought to deal only in facts, for these were the foundation of life. The world was entirely composed of facts: verifiable facts. It was important that boys should learn the creed that the world in its entirety was merely a collection of facts, nothing but facts. Boys should not be encouraged to study magic, fables or fairy folk and should have their minds attuned to the true and verifiable facts of any case. One and one make two, two and two make four, etc. Therein lay the foundation of all knowledge!

By this time, Mrs Coyne had departed this world for her heavenly fairy dell with wild ferns and I had acquired a new mentor – an elderly nun named Sr Magdalene. She had been a Reverend Mother but – as was the convention in the Mercy Order – when she grew older and relinquished her duties as a teacher, she had settled for a place amongst the ordinary sisterhood. Although no longer Reverend Mother, she was still held in great affection with her community of sisters and the wider community of Kells.

The Radio Again

One thing particularly exercised my youthful imagination. It was a conundrum and it had to do with the radio. How did the sound/music/people get into the set in the first place? During years of listening to plays and music, I had developed what was – for me anyway – an entirely satisfactory theory as to how this miracle occurred. The sound could not come from the radio set on its own. Whenever the back of the set was removed to replace a valve, I would be sure to be standing beside my father or the maintenance man. As I could plainly see, the inside of the set was filled mainly with what my father called valves, which to me seemed like strangely shaped bulbs. The workings of the radio innards obviously could not account for how the various sounds got into the radio, to then emerge from the speaker.

Eventually, a theory formed within my head. Like all great theories, it was simplicity itself and offered me great satisfaction. The ingenious formulation went something like this: in order for the radio to respond, it had to be plugged into what the adults called the main supply. It was obvious that all the sounds were coming in through a wire, which entered the set through a tiny hole at the rear. This theory held fast until our parents decided that a new radio set was called for. In due course, it arrived. It was an impressive piece of equipment in that it had a glass dial panel, on which were inscribed about thirty stations, some with exotic and romantic sounding names such as Hilversum and Luxembourg. In the case of the latter, however, I would be entirely disappointed, despite the expectations raised by its name.

The new set was duly plugged in. Immediately the sound poured out. It was just the same, only clearer. The various stations were easier to find. All you had to do was slowly and gently turn the knob. It made a thin line of red move across the dial panel, enabling you to see the name of the station you were looking for. Adding to the mystery of the new technology, Radio Éireann was written onto the dial as Athlone. Amongst the other stations were Hilversum, BBC Light Service, BBC Home Service and of course, The Third Programme.

Everyone breathed a sigh of relief when the new radio performed with so little effort. What was to be done with the old set? It had been discarded for reasons of fashion rather than for any failure to deliver. It was decided to offer the old set to our neighbour, Mr Boland and his family. But I, for one, could not see how it would work – and said so. After all, the Bolands had no mains electricity. There was no way the sounds could enter the set.

The radio in its false mahogany domed case was eventually placed on a table near a window that looked out onto the front garden of the Bolands' Soldiers Cottage. The room in which it sat was referred to as the parlour, a room much less frequented than the kitchen, with its large open fire blazing day after day, summer and winter. To one side of the radio stood two batteries. Boland explained that one was called a dry battery, the other was called the wet battery and had to be brought to a garage every month to be re-charged. It all came down to electricity.

This was a major challenge to my original theory. It completely contradicted the evidence my mind and imagination had assembled that the sound came through the main that connected the radio set to the rest of the world. I felt devastated. The radio that sat alone with its wet and dry batteries on a little table by the Boland's parlour window, was truly a wireless set in the sense that no wires entered from outside.

Then Boland himself unwittingly provided the makings of a new theory as to how this radio worked. He revealed that he brought the wet battery into Jimmy Tobin in the local garage to be re-charged every month. My mind immediately grasped this idea as the basis of the foundation of a new theory. So Jimmy Tobin must be the one who put the sound into the radio. There was nothing special about the battery to look at. It was just a square-shaped glass container, with something looking suspiciously like mere water inside.

As a theory, however, it lacked the convenience of the old. There was now no wire connecting the set to the global network. There was no way the sounds could come filling all the valves before tumbling through the speaker into the room. My inquisitive mind was left confused but not defeated.

Schooling

While continuing my studies with Sr Magdalene, my mind was drawn to another set of objects, which demanded I formulate yet another grand theory of origin. It was one of those glorious, mild spring days, not infrequent in mid-May. Sr Magdalene and I decided that we would take the day's lessons out into the nun's garden. We sat on a bench in a secluded corner, just behind a flowerbed. As we prepared to read my current essay, I noticed about four glass bulbs lying by the edge of the flowerbed.

"Yes, I found those washed up on the shore at Bettystown," Sr Magdalene proffered, in an off-handed dismissive tone. "Fishing boats pass regularly en route from Skerries to Clogherhead."

I understood. The glass globes were floats meant to support fishing nets as they were passed overboard from the trawlers. But my mind – or rather imagination – was racing far ahead of hers. Could sea and tide possibly have moulded those globes by their rocking motion above the sea floor? And why in two colours? One an opaque white and the other bottle green.

So proceeded my elementary education. The Primary Certificate exam was fast approaching for admission to Secondary School. This I looked forward to with both hope and fear in equal amounts. The transformation would be marked by the change from regulation short trousers (which came down to just above the knees), to long trousers (which reached an inch below the ankle). Confirmation was also on the horizon!

Another harbinger of change was the fact that, in the final year of Primary School, two extra subjects were added to the curriculum: History and Geography. These subjects fascinated me, as they seemed to invite both discourse and analysis. Through them, I learnt that for something to be true, there had to be supporting evidence. This method of analysis, I learned much later, was called the empirical method, preferred for all scientific investigation. History was not just stories but based on scientific fact, the foundation of all learning.

Having experienced the satisfaction of vigorous investigation, I now looked forward to Secondary School. Although a strict disciplinary regime still prevailed, my efforts to play my part in the educational process were not dismissed as unrealistic, as they had been in Primary School. I was further encouraged by the inclusion of many new subjects in the Secondary curriculum: subjects such as Church History, which became a big part of Religious Doctrine. And because a second language (Latin) was added to the curriculum, we were obliged to study Roman History. All this was rich nourishment for discourse and speculation.

One thing I can remember vividly is the First Class holding most of its lessons in the Science room, due to a severe shortage of room space. We then had to vacate the room when another year's students had their Science class. The Science room was separated into halves. The bottom half was the one in which most of the experiments were done and was, therefore, bisected by a long worktop, with rows of sinks, water faucets and a Bunsen burner. The top half contained rows of desks, just like any other classroom, except that along the back wall there were shelves filled with every conceivable shape and size of bottle.

One particular bottle I well recall: it was filled with what we later learned to be pure alcohol. On moderately damp days, the glass was slightly clouded. On very dry days it was completely clear. In extremely wet weather the glass was very clouded. Thus, the bottle served as a very accurate barometer of the treatment we might expect from our Science teacher, Brother Arnold, or as a generation of small boys knew him, "Jakesie".

Jakesie was an asthmatic for whom the amount of moisture in the atmosphere was crucial. So every day as we entered class, we glanced anxiously at the very special bottle that stood on a shelf, amidst numerous other bottles of chemicals. If the glass was very clouded Brother Arnold would be unable to leave his sickbed; if the glass was clear we would have nothing to fear, for Brother Arnold would be in the best of health and good spirits, looking forward to a spot of football with the students. On his better days, he fancied himself as a coach. However, the state of his asthmatic condition always had a large bearing on things.

In the classroom, Brother Arnold's favourite scientific experiment was the construction of a mercury barometer, to measure atmospheric pressure and thus predict the weather. We concluded that being an asthmatic, his health depended on moisture and atmospheric pressure. Influence on his frail health was also demonstrated by the bottle of liquid on the shelf. If the bottle completely clouded, he would not be able to teach that day. If partially clouded, he would be in a foul mood. If completely clear, he would be in a good mood and able to picture himself as a successful football manager. All this reminded me of people – especially farming folk – calling to our front door and asking, "Would you ever give the glass a few raps, Sir, and tell me what we can expect now that the grass in the meadow is high and ready to be saved?"

If Brother Arnold happened to be totally indisposed, Mr O'Mahoney would take us for an extra lesson in History or Geography. Now, as I have said, I greatly enjoyed both subjects so you can imagine my disappointment when our teacher delivered his lesson in a long monotone. This was especially true in the case of Geography. Like many of my classmates, I can vividly recall his lessons, especially the one on China, which went something like this: "The Yangste is the largest river in China. Rashers and eggs are rare things. Scarcely a Chinaman knows how to ride a horse."

History lessons were delivered in the same sing-song monotone. Mr O'Mahoney – or "Ducky" as he was known – stubbornly refused to be either shocked by the excesses of the French Revolution, or enthused by the vision of the European Enlightenment. To vary his presentation, he would sometimes crack a feeble joke to relieve the monotony of his lesson. His students always responded with a peel of pretend laughter and cries of, "How very funny!" Ducky would, in desperation, cry out: "Joke over, boys, joke over" but the boys continued with even louder laughter, "But it's very funny, Sir."

He would then glance nervously at his wristwatch, while watching for the appearance of the English teacher, which normally happened just as the laughter was reduced to a mere murmur of merriment. Other teachers must have been very impressed by O'Mahoney's apparent control of his class, and by the enjoyment evident on the boys' smiling faces. Amongst some parents there was, however, concern regarding the kind of education we were receiving.

Ducky was a familiar figure in the town as he made his way from his lodgings in the Royal Meath Hotel to the Secondary School. He was a slightly built – one could even say slightly effeminate – man. Hence the nickname, "Ducky".

Apart from his appearance, another motivation of concern was the fact that Ducky had originally deceived the School Authorities into granting him a permanent position.

Normally, after a year's teaching, a young man was either given such a position or asked to leave, thus exonerating the authorities from having to provide a pension – or other fringe benefits. If, however, a teacher for any reason served more than a year, then he would automatically be given a permanent position. It is said that, his year's contract up, Ducky approached the School authorities to inform them he had secured a position at the North Mons in Cork, but that it would not become vacant until three months hence. If it were alright with the authorities, he would appreciate a short extension to his present contract. This was readily agreed, as it meant that Ducky would be gone in three months' time and his pension rights would become the responsibility of the Christian Brothers at the North Mons.

Well, the three months came and went and then another three months but, each time Ducky was asked about his new job, he simply replied that he was expecting confirmation very soon. The call, however, never came. As month passed into month – and year into year – Mr O'Mahoney became ever more thoroughly ensconced as History and Geography teacher at Kells CBS. He continued to deliver his lessons in the same dull monotone voice; his feeble jokes were still greeted with peals of laughter.

School Friends

I struggled on at school until the eve of the Inter Cert. Then I had to leave, as my fellow pupils were preparing to sit the exam, which was designed to test whether they were fit to eventually attempt the Leaving Cert. Many lucky students already had a career in their sights. Some aspired to become radio officers in the Merchant Navy while others wanted to become cadets in the Defence Forces. One of those who chose the former path would go on to write regular articles for the *Irish Independent*, describing exotic ports he had visited. Of those who went on to be officers in the Defence Forces, many would have their accomplishments reported in the press, especially when Ireland began to play a part in UN peacekeeping services in Congo and the Middle East. By comparison, my life seemed very tame. It could not compare with visiting exotic ports such as Montevideo or Valparaiso. It even compared badly with patrolling the desert sands of the Sinai Peninsula.

My existence was reduced to a small plot in a corner of our large garden, to the rear of our house on the Rockfield Road. Here, I grew cabbage plants to sell to the local populace, mostly farmers wanting a ready supply of greens throughout the year to accompany their thick slices of bacon. Or, perhaps, as autumn and winter approached, a crop that would follow on from the turnips they had grown as a fodder crop, to supplement the feed available for cattle during the long wet winter. A rural prudence taught them the necessity of insuring themselves against harsh weather in January and February.

And so my life went on, not as unpleasantly as one might imagine, for I had always enjoyed working out of doors. Growing cabbage plants for local farmers was not something I had planned doing for the rest of my life. The task of cabbage growing could hardly be classified as an intellectually stimulating occupation. Certainly, it did not stimulate the imagination as much as written composition did for me. The fact of working in the open air provided me with some solace, though not a lot. For, like all boys on the threshold of manhood, I yearned to experience real freedom in a meaningful way.

Many great works of fiction emphasised the fact that freedom was the one, if not the only experience that separated the man from the boy. All true literature – in the best of fiction or non-fiction – held that the most heroic of heroes went to sea. The Robert Louis Stevenson novels: *The Master of Ballintrae* and *Treasure Island*, and radio plays, such as Eugene O'Neill's *Beyond the Horizon*, all proclaimed loudly and clearly that freedom was a boy's inheritance, something gained by going to sea.

Chapter Five:
Knockanally

My mother must have sensed my youthful restlessness since she came up with the idea of sending me to the Rehabilitation Institute at Knockanally near Kilcock, Co Kildare. This was located just outside the Meath border and was then a new venture. It trained young women in secretarial work in its head office off Pearse Street in Dublin, just prior to its move to Leeson Park. Boys and men were trained in leatherwork and watchmaking at different centres scattered throughout the city.

My mother and her sisters were enthusiastic about the whole idea but I was far less so. You could say that I remained downright sceptical to the very last, for I feared that I might be about to be placed in an institution. I worried needlessly on that score. I should have trusted that my mother and known that she would never have placed me in the kind of Institution that plagued my mind.

Knockanally styled itself an Agricultural College. It was surrounded by farmsteads, carved out of an old estate by the Land Commission. Knockanally was attached to the old manor house and was approached via an impressive avenue of trees leading from wrought iron gates, with stone pillars, that formed the entrance. Just inside these elegant gates was an equally elegant little gate lodge, residence of farm manager, Mr Hickey.

Trainees came from all walks of life and educational backgrounds. Some had trained as solicitors or doctors but had dropped out because of the strenuous demands of their calling. Others had come after leaving National School, without having sat their Primary Certificate. These were mostly young men who had contracted polio and spent most of their lives, until then, in Cappagh Hospital. They knew little else other than institutionalised living.

One group of trainees had previously contracted TB. Many had been attended by the eminent Dr Noel Browne. You could see the beneficial effect he had. The former patients absolutely worshipped him: Dr Browne could do no wrong. The Institute – or College as director, Mark Downes liked to call it – was a strange place in those times. Discipline was not overly harsh, except on the occasion of visits from the Rehabs. Institute CEO, Frank Cahill. Then it was all hands to the tiller.

It was the first time that I had ever been away from home and made to stand on my own two feet. At 21 years of age, this felt quite exhilarating and bred a determination never to return to the old structured ways of Irish home life.

At Knockanally, I first came across the idea of physical and mental compensation. Although my physical abilities were not great, it was recognised that I had quite a good brain. The idea of compensation was brought home to me when I encountered a young man from Cork, badly disabled from the waist down, who had managed to develop his upper body to such a degree that, using crutches, he could vault over a 4-foot high fence with an extra drop of two feet on the other side. Everyone waited with bated breath to watch Hickey fly over that fence each morning. As time went on, I would encounter many such examples of triumph in the face of adversity. And in my own life I would, in small ways, under the tutelage of my mother and her sisters, display this facility for mental and physical compensation.

Of course, I also noticed its absence at times, most notably later on during a seminar in Paris, where we were entertained at a hospital for migrant workers who had been severely disabled. Innocently, I raised the subject of mental and physical compensation. The hospital director was not in the least impressed when I asked what rehabilitation and re-training was envisaged for the unfortunate patients. With a wooden smile on his face, he informed me that these men had already given enough in the service of their rural communities. Nothing more ought be asked of them. End of story.

To return to Knockanally!

Every morning, in order to get to the glasshouses, we had to pass through strawberry fields, which stretched down the hill towards our place of work. There were two separate glasshouses: one, a big aluminium structure in eight bays, where the crops were grown and let mature; the other, a single bay constructed in Dutch lights (sheets of glass held in wooden frames). These lights could be used either as cold frames or, as at Knockanally, in the construction of a glasshouse. At the time, Dutch lights were considered revolutionary in glasshouse construction, as their shape allowed in more light than did traditional glasshouses. It was said to be exceptionally beneficial in the construction of what were called, propagation houses. These were normally used for raising seedlings for lettuce and tomato plants, before they were removed to large aluminium-framed outhouses or, as was the case with lettuce plants, to the open ground in the walled garden. The propagation house ran east-west with the result that the plants got light directly from the sun all day long.

The building of the propagation house was completed in late October/early November 1959. It was decided that the first project to be undertaken would be the testing of a soil-less seed and potting compost for Bord na Móna. This was some years before the establishment of the Agricultural Institute at Kinsealy, so Bord na Móna had approached Knockanally's Director, entrusting the college with the task of testing the new soil-less compost under the most rigorous of scientific conditions.

The actual compost had been developed at the State University of California and all the bags bore the large printed letters, UCLA. The compost itself consisted of very fine-grained turf mould with all the consistency of a dark brown mahogany powder. Within each of the bags was a smaller bag of nutrients and trace elements. The bulk of the nutrients were of hoof and horn meal, which were poured over the top of a heap of peat mould, then mixed and wetted on the large concrete apron that fronted the Nissan hut we used as a potting shed. Mixing on the concrete apron could only be completed however on very calm days. As the peat was fine, even a very light breeze would scatter this mould all over the place. When the weather was not considered calm enough, the mixing and wetting of compost was moved into the potting shed.

The first crop to be tested for suitability was one of winter tomatoes. This must have been the first crop of its type in Ireland. The tomato plants were grown in large bitumen pots and fed measured amounts of nutrients. There was a special group of trainees and operatives assigned to measure such things as growth rates, the vigour of the plants and the uptake of nutrients and trace elements but, above all, the ability of the compost to produce a good quality substantial crop. Many of the trials produced much smaller than average fruit. The tomatoes were far sweeter than the average fruit produced for the European markets. This was not a bad thing for, generally in Ireland, as in Europe as a whole, a smaller fruit was preferred. In the USA, the markets seem to prefer a much larger tomato, as exemplified by the names of some of the seed packets – names such as Big Boy. The USA differed dramatically in the type of fruit acceptable to the market. This was demonstrated clearly by the reaction of US visitors to Knockanally. Upon entering the main glasshouse, one such young woman exclaimed in astonishment, "Gosh, you do go in for baby tomatoes."

The propagation house was used to provide growing material for the large aluminium-framed glasshouse, where tomatoes grew in summer, followed in winter by a crop of chrysanthemums. These provided cut blooms for the Christmas trade. Abundant heat was provided from a large square blockhouse, housing a large furnace that was once a ship's boiler, which bore the legend 'John Brown and Co. Glasgow 1911'. This blockhouse was, by any aesthetic standard, an ugly utilitarian building. The scene in the main glasshouses from mid-December to Christmas week was, by contrast, truly a sight to behold, with the serried ranks of blooms in almost every colour that one could imagine, running a gambit all the way from blush pink to brilliant red. To my mind, none could compare with the variety known as Balcombe Perfection, whose petals were of the deepest red, with a reverse sheen on the petal. As the bloom opened, the petals at the centre curled up, exposing their golden undersides. Truly a regal sight – a golden crown on a velvet cushion.

The director had planted, by the side of the boiler house, rows of perennials that he hoped would be the foundation of nursery stock. When the giant hollyhocks and stately delphiniums – not to mention the myriad of other perennials – grew into full bloom, they rivalled the chrysanthemums at Christmas as a sight to behold. Against the southern wall of the blockhouse, the director placed a climbing plant, commonly known as the Cape Gooseberry. It softened the impact of the concrete monstrosity that housed what seemed like the belching innards of a great steam ship.

One of the great advantages Knockanally bestowed on its students was a sense of independence. Most students lived in Dublin and surrounding counties and were allowed go home every second week, and I cannot over-emphasise how much this freedom meant to me personally. To be able to come and go in the world at will was something I very much cherished.

Matron, Mrs Bradley, at Knockanally had arranged with the driver of Kelly's bread van to take me to Kells on alternate weekends. He would pick me up at the college at about 10am on the Friday and drive me to within 500 yards of Doonvarna, the house on the Rockfield road in which my family lived. After the weekend, I would return to Knockanally by catching a bus to Dublin and from there, taking the Galway bus to Kilcock, where it was arranged that I would be picked up at Finn's public house in the centre of the town. Always, when I reached that hostelry, Mrs Finn would have arranged a plate of sandwiches for me in the lounge: an act of kind generosity that always lifted my heart when one considered the bullying and awkward patronising that was usually associated with disability. As I tucked into Mrs Finn's sandwiches, I always hoped that Jack – driver of the college mini-bus – would be delayed, thus shortening my week at Knockanally by a half day.

Other things contributed to strengthening my sense of independence and my development as a person. These included my participation in the activities of community organizations, such as Muintir na Tire, Enfield (one of the stronger guilds in that organization). The Enfield guild was interested in the running of an annual quiz competition during Lent. Why during Lent you may ask? Well, it was a time when all community recreation was banned – or at least seriously circumscribed. Following the dictates of their conscience, the good burghers of Enfield were determined to keep the recreational life of the community functioning in the parish. During the months, February-April the evening light did not allow any meaningful or productive sporting activity. They had to turn to some other form of social intercourse. Question Time was the one they chose. Wisely, they felt this activity answered a social need in a satisfactory way.

For Question Time, two opposing Macra branches would compete in a local hall, where they would be asked general knowledge questions by a Question Master. Elimination rounds were held, leading up to the county finals, which was followed in turn by the regional finals and finally, by the national final.

Macra

The organisation that would have the profoundest effect on me however was Macra na Feirme. My connection with Macra began in 1962, towards the end of my stay at Knockanally. I can vividly remember, to this day, a group of us students being driven in the college mini-bus to the parish hall at Newtown, on the back road to Enfield. Although this hamlet liked to style itself a village, it was really no more than a collection of four or five scattered houses, a church and a shop.

Two of the houses had been gutted and reconstructed as a parish hall. One evening, we attended a meeting at Newtown because the new Macra branch there proposed to pick a team to compete in the National Debating Competition. They wished to expand the base of people from which they could choose. In their wisdom, the branch officers had decided to invite some Knockanally trainees to audition for a place on the debating team.

Knockanally director, Mark Downes and the Newtown branch chairman would select the team. The topic for debate was, "The establishment of a national TV service was long overdue."

In his summing up of the debate, Downes remarked, with a wry smile on his face, that he was surprised that those of us who favoured the setting up of a national station appeared to have concentrated on the dangers of foreign domination of the cultural airwaves. Were the cultural values of BBC Northern Ireland and Ulster TV all that different to the values of the Irish nation? he asked. After all, we had only to look at the broad output of Radio Éireann to see that our values were not at risk of domination, certainly not from Ulster TV or anything in the Six Counties. Although my contribution to the debate was something of a disaster, to say the least, another of the students from Knockanally was selected to be a member of the Newtown Macra debating team: one Kevin Bracken by name. Kevin was a very intelligent man and very much at ease as a debater, a skill which he must have acquired as a student at Roscrea. Another of the local men, Peter Maguire, was a noted Kildare footballer (at a time when football meant something in Kildare) who also happened to work as a horticultural foreman in Knockanally.

The Newtown Macra branch did, after many vigorous debates, reach the county finals. This was no mean achievement for a branch then barely two months in existence. I recall the motion for debate at the county final: "That Ireland should apply to become the 51st state of the USA."

This was a fairly topical notion, in that both Hawaii and Alaska had recently applied to become the 49th and 50th states respectively of the USA. The team proposing the motion dwelt on the strength of family and kinship ties between Ireland and the USA, not to mention the growing economic ties that would come to bind the two nations even closer together.

The whole debate was conducted in a tone of extreme moderation and well-mannered orderliness. That was until Kevin Bracken opened for the opposition on a humorous note, although that humour was not appreciated by everyone in the hall. He told the story of Noah and his ark. Kevin related how, when the ark was a mere few days on the flood, the bull that occupied the stern of the boat was already defecating profusely. Noah sensed that there was a serious problem here: that one half of the bovine duo on board was emitting at such a rate as to pose a risk to the ark itself. Noah, however, held off tackling the problem until he perceived that the stern of the boat was sinking in the waters and the prow rising. He could see that strong measures were called for. If the craft capsized, that would be the end of the world and every living thing on it.

Noah approached the bull, who expressed a willingness to clear out the bovine accommodation but complained that there were insufficient implements on board to do it safely and cleanly. Noah pointed out that elephants had been provided by nature with the very implements needed, so he approached them and they reluctantly agreed, while insisting that the bull must also play his part. Meanwhile, the Ark had come to a stop above what is now called Manhattan. The job was then commenced. A day later, the manure rose above the surface of the waters. Kevin then asked rhetorically, "Do we really want to be tied to such a load of old bull?"

Some members of the audience expressed only a little unease at the reference to a load of old bull but the more prudish and humourless took grave exception to this reference. It did not, however, faze the judges at all. They awarded the county championship to Newtown.

This was astonishing in that the branch was barely two months in existence. The judges had decided, nevertheless, that the branch could proceed to the inter-county finals in the competition. Although Newtown was beaten by a more experienced team, it did extremely well for a new branch.

Meanwhile, an attractive young schoolteacher, who had been a member of Enfield guild of Muintir na Tire, came calling, accompanied by her father. She had seen me win the Enfield Guild's Question Time competition and had decided to call on the off chance that I would be in. As it so happened, I was sitting on a seat outside the entrance to the big house at Knockanally. With me was my friend, Bernard (Benny) Boyle. When the pretty young school mam and I set off on a walk together, Benny decided to tag along. As we approached the pride of the centre – the glasshouses – I felt a mix of emotions. I knew that I had made a favourable impression on the young woman but was angry that Ben should have invited himself along.

Kevin Bracken was even angrier than I was with Benny for butting into what was obviously a social visit. No matter how I felt – or how others felt for me – my friendship with Benny Boyle survived nonetheless. We would be involved in various scrapes together.

The most notable involved the aforementioned Peter Maguire, Kildare inter-county footballer and foreman of horticulture at the centre. This involved our borrowing Peter's pride and joy – his blue Renault – for a spin. As things turned out, this was to prove a very expensive spin for me. Having traversed the grounds of Knockanally estate, we left the Renault back at the place at which we had found it, in the sure – though mistaken – belief that no one had seen us come or go. How mistaken we were! We had in fact been seen leaving the car back. Peter Maguire was obviously told and brought his car to the local garage. Here a fault was detected in the engine. The cost of correcting the damage was estimated at £45, which I had to pay as Benny had no funds.

The publicity surrounding this incident exceeded the gravity of the incident itself. What I found most strange and alarming was the number of people who approached me to suggest I should blame the whole affair on Benny Boyle. According to my boyish sense of honour, this was something I could not do. Kevin Bracken was one of the most insistent that I blame Benny. I could see his point, nevertheless, it seemed more important to remain loyal to a friend at all costs.

Throughout my subsequent career, especially when it came to the governance of organisations for which I had a responsibility, I always saw loyalty to others as the primary principle to be observed. I regarded loyalty and trust to be the highest virtues.

Another student, with whom I became very friendly was one Frank Southwood. Our friendship got off to a very sticky start. In fact, I can say without contradiction that we took an instant dislike to one another. That was until after the row in the coach-house. And what a row it was: violent and very physical. The tension between us had been building up for a number of weeks. So enraged were both of us that people were quite clearly keeping out of our way. Foremen, instructors and trainees were obviously avoiding us in the knowledge that a storm was about to break.

It is no wild country superstition that all animals – especially the fowl of the air – know a storm is brewing in that deathly silence before it breaks. There is a hush, as if everything has come to a standstill. It was the same kind of blind country knowledge that warned instructors and outside labourers of an impending row. As the storm approached, they withdrew from the coach-house, while continuing to keep watch through cracks in the wooden door.

Frank and I circled, pursuing one another around a heap of animal feed in the centre of the coach-house floor. Each was determined not to be the one who struck the first blow: but equally determined not to be the one who suffered the shock of the initial thrust. In spite of my lack of physical strength it was I who struck the first blow. Frankie lost his balance and fell backwards into a mound of animal feed. The blow came as a shock to him, he confided later. It might have been a shock to him but it was an even bigger one to me.

I watched him lying in a heap of animal feed, bruised in spirit if not in body. I grew fearful but strangely powerless to call a halt to the fight. And so it continued for some time, with neither of us being the one to throw in the towel. I, for one, had no idea what this desperate fight was all about. Only the feeling surged through my body: a feeling of hostile resentment towards Frank. I have little doubt that he experienced the same rush of distracted emotions. Frankie slowly rose from the bed of meal and trace elements destined for the pigs. When he got to his feet, he rushed at me. His clenched fist connected with my face. I felt a sharp stinging pain as I fell backward into some other pile of animal feed. Thus, it continued, each of us in turn ending up lying in the bed intended for the college's prize pigs.

As we tired, the pace of combat slowed considerably, the two of us were completely exhausted – both physically and mentally. Both of us finished up lying in beds of animal feed. An eerie, though strangely expectant, silence reigned. Only then did those who kept watch through the cracks in the door start to show themselves. The bolt of the door was pulled back as men and boys drifted in, many on tiptoes out of fear or respect. No one spoke. The older men, the instructors and some of the day labourers shook their heads wearily and knowingly, as they held out their hands in turn to each of us – the two fallen heroes.

It was, for all the world, like an episode from *The Annals of Ulster* or the *Iliad*. The older and wiser men pulled each of us onto our feet and, with their broad farmers' hands gently brushed our clothes and faces, while still nodding to one another sagely. The two of us were then brought together face-to-face. Hesitantly, I held out my hand to Frankie, who grasped it warmly. I, in turn, tightened my grip on his extended hand. Frank smiled. The storm had died. Catharsis had been achieved. All the hostility and suspicion we had harboured towards one another melted away. We became firm friends.

We would explore the city of Dublin together, in search of its more fashionable waterholes and salubrious restaurants. One of our frequent haunts was a restaurant-cum-wine bar, The New Amsterdam. Shades of Greenwich Village! The bar had, according to Frankie, acquired a reputation for having an exotic and slightly risqué clientele. Exotic though it may have been The New Amsterdam would close within a year. Because of its exotic reputation? I doubt it. I suspect the 'exotic' clientele was a figment of Frankie's powerful imagination.

Another student with whom I became very friendly was one Paul Sheridan. I visited him at his parents' house on the Navan Road in Dublin. Paul had studied medicine for a short time at the Royal College of Surgeons but his health broke down and he had to give up all thoughts of a medical career.

His mother was a retired schoolteacher. She came from somewhere outside Mullingar. His father was born in Argentina, one of the thousands of Irish Midlands emigrants who had put down roots in that country. It was jokingly said that they spoke Spanish with a strong Mullingar accident, though for the life of me, I can still not figure out how one can distinguish Spanish spoken with a Mullingar accent, or with any other accent for that matter.

Interestingly, Che Guevara came from a similar Irish background. But our Paul was unlike Che and other students in that he was no revolutionary. When not working in the glasshouse, he dressed in dark suits. Even the red pullover he habitually wore under his jacket came out black whenever a photo was taken. This often led the observer of the photograph to ask who the clerical student was. This query infuriated Paul, especially when it came from young women.

Another thing that tended to mark out Paul as somewhat conservative was the fact that, as a smoker, his choice of cigarette brand was Senior Service. When he failed to secure an adequate supply of them, he would have to settle for Players Navy Cut.

Yet another contemporary at Knockanally was an impressive young man from Wexford, named Matt Sharpe. I particularly remember him as a prime example of what I call physical and mental compensation. Due to an attack of infantile polio, he had the use of only one arm but this did not prevent him from performing all the functions necessary for a normal life: such as dressing himself. This extraordinary ability to function normally was exemplified by an incident after Matt began taking driving lessons. Before the first lesson, the instructor questioned Matt's ability to drive a car when, presumably, he could not even tie his own shoelaces. Matt responded by bending down, untying his laces then retying them within seconds using only the one hand. A look of amazement covered the instructor's face. Matt only smiled and enquired whether the instructor would like him to remove his necktie.

"Oh no," replied the embarrassed instructor, "I think you have shown me enough."

So began Matt's first driving lesson.

The end of my time at Knockanally drew closer. I found myself growing more and more restless. I looked to putting into practice social and other skills I had learnt at the centre. One of these involved getting a part-time job, which turned out to be selling football pools. It would sustain me while I tried to build a business, propagating black currant bushes for the newly formed Erin Foods; then under the charismatic leadership of General Michael Joe Costello.

Forward more than fifty years. On Sunday, 1 June 2014, I took a trip back in time to research facts for this volume of memoirs. The house and grounds I knew as Knockanally Agricultural and Horticultural Training Centre had been converted into a golf course. The strange thing about visiting the locations and sources of our deepest memories are that spaces are inclined to appear smaller and more crowded. At Knockanally, the archway entrance to the farmyard had been preserved and the entrance to the chicken loft could be recognized up a flight of stone steps. At the edge of a fairway now stands a narrow, wrought iron gate, framed in the original stone and brick of a wall enclosing a four-acre garden, which used to be filled with lettuce in the spring and chrysanthemums in the late summer and autumn. Most of the wall is now gone: only a rear section bordering one of the back fairways remained intact.

As I gazed across the fairway, at what I took to be the front wall of the garden, a young man detached himself from a group of his golfing comrades. Walking towards me with outstretched hands, he greeted me with a handshake, his face all the while remaining expressionless. Suddenly, remembering where I was and why I had come, the word 'disability' flashed into mind. It was obvious the young man had Tourette's syndrome. As I walked back along the fairway, I could see through the filter of memory that the place now seemed crowded. I then ascended a slight incline to the main house, where two years of my life was spent over 50 years ago. That house is now the golf course clubhouse. Prior to serving as the Rehabs. Centre, the house was one of many owned by the Maharajah of Burundi.

Having decided to dine in the clubhouse, my companion and I entered what was, 50 years ago, the TV room of the training centre: now serving as bar-cum-dining room for the clubhouse. The office, where two trainee clerks, Randall Counihan and Brendan Stapleton, used to hold forth, had been joined to the former TV room to make the present day lounge bar. Despite the addition of the office however, the room seemed smaller than I had remembered it. And, of course, it seemed more crowded. For one thing, there was now a lot more furniture.

We seated ourselves near the window that once over-looked the centre's garden and lawns, where director Mark Downes had set up a pitch-and-putt course. Beyond the course, the strawberry field fell all the way down to where the glasshouses once were. The field itself was now planted with trees, to establish natural obstacles for the golf course, which came to within 20 paces of the present-day clubhouse. The meal was excellent: the lasagne and the chunky chips just delicious. My companion enjoyed an open chicken sandwich. The meal, drinks included, came to a mere €30.

We then set off on a tour of locations outside the grounds of Knockanally. The first was the half-parish of Newtown, where we students used attend Mass in the chapel all that long time ago. Newtown village had then consisted of a chapel, shop and dwelling house, along with a small National School and half a dozen sturdy farmhouses. To me, the village now looked spectacularly different. Unlike Knockanally, no markers remained to remind me of past days. There was nothing to harness the power of memory or imagination. The dwelling house and school had been combined to form a community centre. Over the door of the former schoolhouse had been erected a plaque in honour of Teresa Brayton, local schoolmistress, songwriter and author of the popular ballad, *The Old Bog Road*. The small church had been replaced by a large modern one, obviously built in the late 70s or early 80s. Inside seats were arranged in a semi-circular fashion, like an amphitheatre, rendering it much more spacious.

As students in the early 60s, we'd argued about the future of the Church and its chances of survival, while at the same time attending to our religious duties. It was as if we were living through a lengthy grey twilight before the inevitable fall. All the while, unbeknownst to us, the Church had been striving to bring the Knockanally Institute into its orbit.

As I mentioned earlier, one of the most beneficial consequences of the two-year stay at Knockanally was my introduction to Macra na Feirme and its activities. At that time – the early 1960s – the National Headquarters was at Athy, Co. Kildare. It later moved to Northumberland Road, Dublin 4 and later again, to Bluebell, Dublin 8. The fact that the HQ was once based in Kildare helps explain Macra's continued popularity in that county.

Macra enabled me to travel all over western Europe, to take part in conferences and other meetings, none of which passed without controversy. One was a proposed trip to Cuba by the Youth Federation of Ireland, whose leader at the time was one Dermot Lacey, now for many years a Labour councillor in Dublin 4. This was a cause of much concern to the leadership of the Catholic Scouts and Girl Guides of Ireland. Ireland was, however, changing by the late 60s and most of the constituent organizations had higher priorities than the issue of travel to some small island state. At the time, Macra had only just re-joined the Youth Council of Ireland, a return facilitated in part by Fergal O'Farrell, a member of the Young Methodists.

Fergal was to make so many trips across the city to Macra HQ at Bluebell, Inchicore and become so impressed with the ethos of our organization that he would join as a member of staff, with the title of Adult Education Officer. His brother, Fergus, became an advisor to the late George Birmingham, Minister of State in the Fitzgerald-led coalition government in the 1980s. Another man who would play a vital part in Macra, as education officer, was Tom Collins, later director of Dundalk Institute of Technology and later again, Professor of Sociology at Maynooth.

My mother, Annabel Lee, aged 16

My father, John Lee, in RIC dress uniform, aged about 27 years

My father, John Lee, with me in his arms

Myself, sister Mairéad and brother John

Myself, sister Mairéad, brother John and family pets

Myself and brother John
in 1958 (the year he left
for the USA)

In our front garden.
Rear: My brother John and
myself.
Front: My sister Mairéad
and mother

Myself, Marie Rourke (Kells) and Helen McGovern (Navan) at *Poets for Africa* function on board the MV Aran on the River Liffey, Dublin, August 1986

Myself c. 2012

Family group at Hurdlestown, Kells c. 1940
Rear (L-R): Uncle Richie Lee, father John Lee, uncle Dennis Lee
Middle (L-R): Cousin Paddy Martin, grandmother Annie Lee,
cousin Molly Martin
Front (L-R): Cousins Noel Martin and John Martin
(sons of my aunt Katie)

Knockanally House, Kildare. Formerly Rehabilitation Institute agricultural training centre, now club house for Knockanally golf course

Cafe and film museum Potsdam, formerly royal stables for the Hollenzollerns

Garrison church of the Hollenzollerns, Potsdam

The Di Fabrik Café, Berlin

Chapter Six:
Business Activities

After I left Knockanally, it was envisaged for a time that I might become an organiser for the Rehab Pools. This would have involved my income being split between a small salary and a generous commission. It would have entailed driving a car but my body coordination was, to say the least, not great. So that put an end to any idea of becoming a pools organiser or fundraiser. I would have to content myself with being a mere collector. This involved much walking, especially when I had to call on houses two, or even three, times. The income from the pools did, nonetheless, help sustain me, or at least keep me in pocket money. I continued to progress by degrees.

Meanwhile, on the horticultural front, things also progressed slowly. To the rear of the family house in Kells, we built a cold frame fitting it out with soil-warming cables so that I could raise lettuce seedlings in it. To the frame was added a long narrow steel sash glasshouse, 6' x 24'. In the frame, I raised seedlings of all kinds, which I then pricked out and grew in trays before transferring them to the open ground. My smallholding gradually developed into a general nursery.

In May, June and July each year, I sold spring and summer bedding as well as lettuce plants. And for most of the year, I raised, for sale, a diversity of brassica plants: york, savoy, curly kale, Brussels sprouts and cauliflowers. And, along with these members of the broccoli family, I recall the garden being used primarily to supply the house with fresh vegetables.

A plan to propagate blackcurrant bushes for sale to commercial growers came to nothing. My uncle, Richie, who was a farmer, was to join me in this venture but suddenly got cold feet. He gave as his reason that as an old man, he could not be expected to keep up with a young man, albeit a disabled one. Within the family, however, it was suspected that the real reason for his failure of nerve was that, just a few years previously, he had been persuaded by the local Horticultural Instructor to invest in the creation of a small commercial orchard but the project never created the revenues expected. This had apparently left Uncle Richie with a deep sense of failure.

After the failure of the blackcurrant project to materialise, I fell in with a landholding shopkeeper, who had some land on the Rockfield Road near our house. We planned on growing the lettuce plants I had raised in my cold frame. The local farmer, who had ploughed the acre or so of land in preparation for my tender, was highly sceptical of our project, comparing the micro-climate in the Kells area unfavourably with that of the coastal districts of North County Dublin. This project soon came to grief when the local shopkeeper came to realise just how much hard manual labour was involved in large-scale, out-of-season production.

One of the things about memory is that it brings up interesting images. At the beginning of my career, there was a nursery product, a hedging plant called *Cupressus macrocarpa*, which as a species, unfortunately, grew too high, making it unwieldy in windy conditions. It was commonly described as a weed. We in the nursery trade made every effort to find a substitute and thought we had found it in *Leylandii cypress*. This turned out to be a rather dull looking hedge. We later tried to use a plant called *Castlewellan Gold*, which originated in Co. Down. It was golden yellow, fast growing and easy to clip.

A man called David Robinson, managing director of a consortium of nurseries in the North, encouraged us in its use. *Castlewellan Gold* however, also proved unsuitable. It may be seen to this day in badly mottled hedges that have been attacked by aphids: for example, at the parochial house at Dunshaughlin. Growing conifers is a risky business. I have known plants imported for their diminutive size eventually grow to 10-15 feet. *Cypress boulevarde* is an example. This is just one perspective of plant production that memory provides.

Macra Again

About a year after leaving Knockanally, I renewed my acquaintance with Macra na Feirme. It all began with a talk given in the local vocational school in Kells. Following the presentation, a discussion took place on setting up a branch in the town. One of the students who spoke was James Newman, a local student of rural science (which included the skill of welding). James would become the first chairman of the new branch and subsequently, National Representative. This made him a member of the governing council of Macra. Later again, he would become National Honorary Secretary. In the following years, this was to become something of a pattern for Kells branch members: first membership of the National Council, then the National Executive, then the position of National Honorary Secretary. Indeed, three of the four local members who became national reps, went on to occupy the position of National Honorary Secretary: James Newman, then myself, then Kevin Brady.

I was not a year back in Macra when I was asked to take part in coaching Question Time, Public Speaking and Debating teams. At the time, Macra's function was to train young farmers for leadership in organisations such as the IFA and, of course, political parties. Debating and public speaking were considered the most important competitions, with the highest educational and training content.

In reality, Macra was a social, cultural and educational body. Question Time encouraged you to enhance your store of general knowledge, while debating and public speaking allowed you to hone your skills in what we call communications and advocacy. The plan was that skills thus acquired, would help young farmers to play their part in the development of their industry, especially in the political/economic arena. This type of training lasted some years, right up until the advent of *Telefís na Feirme*. This was a farming programme presented by Justin Keating, then lecturer in Veterinary Science at TCD. The programme presented a set of practical farming skills in a very professional manner. But debating and public speaking remained key pillars of Macra training and education. I was also enlisted as a coach, not only for these teams but for the Question Time team as well.

The next big Macra competition was the new quiz for television. This was called *Cross Country Quiz* and was chaired by Liam Mullally. Peter Murphy of Macra headquarters was the scorekeeper. It featured teams from all over the country, competing to become the overall champions. In the first year of the competition, Donal Black, who ran a small but successful garden centre on the Dublin Road outside Drogheda, was the team coach. The following year I took over that role.

This high-profile competition did not find favour with all in the organization however, despite the fact that the publicity would benefit Macra as a whole: and despite the fact that Macra scorekeeper, Peter Murphy, had been voted TV personality of the year by the general public. After two years, the programme was discontinued, so something had to be devised that would involve branch members in each county. The answer to this conundrum came in the shape of a proficiency competition. Such competitions were essentially regional in appeal, involving about 14 separate competitions throughout the county. Two or three counties participated in each. Instead of engaging just a few members – three to six – the competition involved the entire branch. Each winter and spring, the branches busied themselves in devising projects. This consisted mainly of planning a business start-up or conducting a survey on how to deliver social services to the local community, in as efficient a manner as possible.

Young, practising farmers continued to be the mainstay and chief concern of the organization, another 20-30% of the membership –although coming from a farming background – did not earn their living directly from either agriculture or horticulture. These included bank and council officials working locally. This type of young person was the mainstay of social, cultural and sporting activities in most small and medium-sized towns on the prosperous east coast and in the Midlands. Members of Macra – or Young Farmers as they were collectively known – provided a focal point around which other young people could gather for leisure and recreation.

Why should this be the case? Were there no other social outlets for would be Macra members? Well, the GAA did not suit everyone. And every town of any substantial size had its sports clubs (such as tennis and rugby) but these catered primarily to the commercial classes: anyway, most young men would have joined more than the one club. Macra added to the range of recreational activities on offer. Those who took part and were willing to put in an effort, generally gained fulfilment and advanced themselves. I can think of four or five of our members who either joined the civil service or became local government officials.

My own involvement led to much opportunity for travel. Head Office would regularly ring me of a Monday to know whether I could be in Strasbourg, Amsterdam, Paris or Brussels by Friday. If my answer was yes, a ticket would promptly arrive in the post. The first conference I attended, however, took place at University College Galway and seemed rather mundane at first.

The year was 1962. The event was a cross border initiative but there was no friction between members of the nationalist and unionist communities present. This was the time of the Civil Rights movement in the North. There were a number of interesting speakers, some from the Free Derry enclave. The subject of the conference, if my memory serves me right, was community development and local participatory democracy. The Macra delegation comprised two staff members – Paul Grisewood and John Murphy (both education officers at HQ) – and myself. We warmed to the subject as we listened to speaker after speaker. I well remember a young lecturer from Manchester University. He was both professional and eloquent. As the conference progressed, we managed to gather a group around us. We attracted people from all walks of life and all kinds of background.

Chapter Seven:
Europe

The feeling of being empowered was obvious to me at Galway. Would I feel the same if I attended conferences and seminars in mainland Europe? It certainly did on one such occasion: a conference in 1973 at Strasbourg, in a centre close to the newly built European Parliament building. It involved representatives from most of the states of the European Economic Community (EEC) as it was known at the time.

This was a time of great change, both within Ireland and in Europe as a whole. The Government of the Republic was, it seems, beginning to grapple with the thorny issue of birth control, having ignored the subject for years. In 1973, the EEC undertook its first accession – adding Ireland, Britain and Denmark to the original six countries. And within a couple of years, the fascist regime of Caetano in Portugal had fallen to the Carnation Revolution, while in neighbouring Spain, Franco had died.

The venue for our seminar was the Cynac Building, which stood just across the river from the Parliament Building in Strasbourg. The building was fronted with copper-tinted glass. The building was not pretty, proclaiming as it did, its post-war modernist utilitarianism. Less than three decades after the end of World War II, Europe had been re-drawing and re-building itself in order to take advantage of the newfound opportunities of the EEC, as it was taking shape before our eyes: a united Europe offering us everlasting peace and undisputed prosperity. The last of the right-wing dictators had gone without a drop of blood being spilt. Throughout Europe, autocracy was giving way to democracy. The resurrected monarchy in Spain – intended to copperfasten the continuing rule of the Falangists – had evolved, in fact, into a constitutional monarchy, not all that different from their northern European counterparts.

At the commencement of the Strasbourg conference, the convenor stated that he had been surprised by the letter he was about to read out. It was from an organisation not in attendance and questioned the right of another organisation to represent that country. The latter was, in fact, a boy scouts organisation that was in attendance. It was obvious that the objectors represented the last remnants of the former Salazar-Caetano regime. Regardless of this challenge, the young boy scouts from Lisbon proved extremely helpful to the rest of us at the conference, assisting us with slides and acetate projections. This was in sharp contrast to those who came to the conference representing Portugal's larger neighbour, Spain. These young Spaniards advertised their left-wing leanings. I can well remember, in particular, one heavily made up young woman, whom we came to call La Passionaria, after the heroine of the Spanish Civil War.

The southern Italians seemed to fall in ideologically with the vociferous Spaniards. In the case of La Passionaria, it was obvious that she was reacting to forty years of oppression by the Franco dictatorship: a reaction later explained to me by another young Spanish woman some twenty years later, as we breakfasted together in the Church of Ireland hostel at Sandymount in Dublin. "You must realise that the dictatorship was the dullest and most depressing epoch in the entire history of Spain, fuelled by a hunger for respectability amongst the nations."

For those unfamiliar with Europe as a cultural and political entity, Strasbourg sounded as though it were a German city. There were many innocents abroad in the late 70s – not a few of them from Ireland – who thought it was a German city. In fact, it lies on the French side of the post-World War II border. The Strasbourg Conference was concerned with broad aspects of the development of the European Union.

There were delegates from every corner of the continent – except the Eastern bloc – from Scandinavia and Southern Europe for the most part. Spain and Portugal, I have already mentioned but smaller states included Cyprus and Malta. Strasbourg was also memorable because it was the first time I came into contact with the Greens. Coming as I did from Ireland, green, when applied to anything political, could only mean nationalism – particularly a narrow and blinkered form of nationalism. These people, however, were not Green in the Irish nationalist sense, but Environmentalists!

To go back a bit however, myself and fellow delegate Patsy McClean arrived about ten days in advance of the conference. A mistake had been made in Brussels – or perhaps in the Macra office in Dublin. It meant that Patsy and I had ten days in which to explore the city before getting down to work. As we had arrived early, no arrangements had been made for feeding us. We had, however, been issued with money to buy food in eating-places outside the conference centre. So we dined every evening at a nearby restaurant, mostly on cheese-and-beef burgers. At the time these were not so common in Ireland, as it was thought that cheese would dilute the taste of good prime beef. But it suited me, since I liked both beef and cheese. For my fellow delegate, it was a case of sticking with what you know. He knew from boyhood that burgers were safe. He nevertheless asked me to tell him if I caught him eating snails. I told him that he could eat anything except food labelled 'escargots'. Patsy smiled knowingly and said, "Glad to be warned of the signs of an offending dish."

His smile was as broad as that of a schoolboy on learning that a Diet of Worms was not what the name implied but rather, a provincial German parliament. Such are the delightful vagaries of language, if not the singular nature of the German character.

Another example of differing national characteristics surfaced at this conference. This time however, it involved differences within a national camp – the Swedes. The conference was only a few hours old when a handsome young couple announced themselves as members of the Green Party and part of the Swedish delegation. The young woman was named Honor and, as far as I can remember, the young man was called Jorge. The other half of the Swedish delegation was composed of Social Democrats. Honor and Jorge had many complaints about the Social Democrats, mainly concerning their arrogance. They complained that they were stuffing the cubby holes of every delegation with Social Democrat propaganda. The Social Democrats tried to pass off the stuffing of cubby holes as a joke, even trying to dismiss the Green movement as some kind of joke or aberration.

Beneath all the bluster, you could see clearly that the Social Democrats were fearful of the Greens. They feared any opposition coming from the Left. It was not hard to see why they would resent these newcomers to Scandinavian politics. For almost a century, the Social Democrats had been the prime movers and shapers of Swedish democracy, with their belief in neutrality abroad and equality and social justice at home. The highly commendable ideals of social justice and democracy were pursued by the ruling party with the thoroughness of the northern political culture to which they belonged. The Greens acted in accord with similar ideals.

Difference within yet another delegation surfaced, this time between the two Swiss delegates. I hasten to add that there was no open hostility between the two, though each tried his hardest to outdo the other in argument. The two men had totally different perceptions of the political system in their home country. One came from the French-speaking part of the Federation and the other from the German-speaking part. The German-speaking delegate spoke highly of the Swiss system of rule by plebiscite, while his fellow delegate – a student who hailed from the Jura (predominantly French-speaking and one of the poorest cantons in the country) – argued that rule by plebiscite was anything but democratic. By way of example, he cited how banks manipulated the system. If the legislature passed a law that bank executives felt was not in their best interest, they would organise a petition calling for a plebiscite to overturn the law. When the plebiscite was held, the banks and other financial institutions would make serious and successful efforts to ensure all their employees went out and voted in accordance with their employers' wishes. It must be remembered that, put together, the financial institutions were the largest employers in Switzerland. The German-speaking delegate spoke eloquently about the system of Swiss governance. In his opinion, it was one of the finest examples of democratic government to be found in Europe – or anywhere. What other system could integrate populations of French and German speakers, working for the common good of their mountainous nation?

He also mentioned Switzerland's achievement as the nation that produced the cuckoo clock. Nothing could disturb the tranquillity of these industrious peoples, save for the hourly insistence of said clock. The delegate from the Jura declared that he deemed it a privilege to have met myself and Patsy McClean. Needless to say, this went down well with us.

Yet another delegate we got to know very well was a member of the British team, a Cockney. He informed us that he hailed from London, from somewhere close to the Thames. Upriver from where he resided, silicon had been discovered amongst the more numerous shale deposits: so the future seemed very bright in the age of computers.

The conference dealt with all forms of economic development, ranging from computers to banking. Patsy and I focused our contributions on the agricultural sector of the Irish economy, which was then practically the whole economy. We were, after all, supposed to be representing the young farmers of Ireland. We highlighted the growth in cereal production and the consequent changes this form of agricultural production had wrought on the landscape. Hedgerows had been ripped out as smaller fields gave way too much larger ones and herds of lowing cattle had given way to the golden harvest, creating an Irish version of the silicon shale that had become the hope of Thames Valley residents.

Those are my memories of Strasbourg. My next outing was when I represented the Irish Young Farmers at a conference held in Paris, on the subject of health and social protection in Europe. It was convened by the OECD and included states such as Cyprus and Malta, which were not part of the EEC. The Irish delegation of which I was part, included three civil servants – two men and a woman. One of the men was an official working in the department of then Minister of Health and Social Welfare, the renowned CJ Haughey. The agenda for the conference covered the entire gamut of social and medical policy. I represented the Young Farmers but the delegation as a whole was led by a Mr Tom Llewelyn of the IFA. The high point was a visit to a hospital at Le Mans, which catered for farm workers from all over France who had acquired injuries in the course of their working lives. It was obvious many had very serious head injuries, as their heads were clamped into rests for support. The patients were marshalled on stage as if to make clear the theme of their extreme dependency. Accompanying them was the medical director. His demeanour suggested an inordinate pride in his institution – and the quality of care it delivered. He waxed lyrical on the subject of the care that his hospital afforded these "poor wretches". His words not mine!! There was no mention of rehabilitation or capacity building, let alone independence.

Following his speech, the discussion was thrown open to contributions from the floor. As a disabled young man, I felt an acute surge of anger within me. All my childhood and teenage experiences came flooding back to me: all the coping I had learned from my mother, sister, brother, aunts and cousins. The phrase I had so often rehearsed immediately sprung to my mind: 'Mental and physical compensation'.

Glorious to behold, this phenomenon was integral to the development of a sense of independence for a person with disability. I had experienced this compensatory effect at work in my own life: for example, the development of my spoken English to a high standard to compensate for my bad handwriting.

I stood up at the hospital seminar and set forth my position. The medical director came to the front of the stage and expressed his astonishment that more should be asked of the "poor wretches". According to the director, these men had acquired their injuries in the course of their work. The duty we owed them was one of extreme care. They should not want for anything. Their meagre wishes should be satisfied without complaint but with great satisfaction. The director's remarks were withering and intended to be so but I had not finished. When the plenary session commenced the next morning, I raised the question again, having weighed it up in my mind overnight. I was now able to formulate it in more eloquent terms and managed to get my point across quite forcibly.

*   *   *

I continued to visit the continent on a fairly regular basis. I recall one of the early trips, a session held at the Folk High School at Ardensberg, in the south of Holland. It was winter, December to be precise. Although everyone claimed it was a mild winter, a heavy frost lay on the surrounding fields. Ardensberg was a hamlet joined to other hamlets to form a municipality. In the municipal offices, we were treated to sherry and St Nicholas's Staff, a sweet bread filled with marzipan and intended to be seen as part of a bishop's staff (that of St Nicholas – or Santa Claus – who journeyed from Spain to Holland with his servant, Black Peter).

The Ardensberg outing commenced on a very uncertain note. I arrived at Dublin airport only to discover that my flight to London (from where I was to take a connecting flight to Brussels) had already left. Someone had put the wrong departure time on my ticket. To add to the confusion there was no sign of my fellow Macra delegate, Joe Doyle, who hailed from Bunclody, Co. Wexford. Myself and a friend, Kevin Brady who had driven me to the airport held a quick confab. We decided that I should continue on my way to London, reasoning that I could always sleep on a seat at Heathrow that night, before proceeding to Brussels the next morning. When I was already in the air, on the next available flight, I decided to tell the cabin stewardess of my predicament, showing her my ticket and indicating my intention to sleep on an airport bench.

"That's not possible. No staying at the airport overnight," she insisted.

She took away my ticket but later returned to inform me that, since the mistake was made at the airline office, she had arranged for me to stay at a Trust House Forte Hotel. A courtesy coach would collect me at Heathrow and deliver me to the hotel. Upon arrival at the hotel, I was treated to an open turkey sandwich that was very satisfying, being more meat than bread. Needless to say, I slept well that night. I arose early next morning, breakfasted and was driven by coach back to the airport.

I successfully boarded my Brussels flight and, within 20-30 minutes, we were making our descent. Emerging from the customs hall, I made my way to an underground station and caught a train to Central Station, then crossed the street to the bus station, where a bus to Ardensberg had been arranged for conference delegates. I was happy with the thought that I would probably run into someone else on their way to the conference. As I reached the station entrance, I encountered a group of men conversing together in some foreign language other than French. After a few moments eavesdropping, it suddenly dawned on me that these men were speaking Welsh. They informed me they were sheep farmers from North Wales and that they were, indeed, on their way to Ardensberg.

As we were talking, who should pass by, only my friend Joe Doyle. I hailed him in English by his Christian name. He looked around startled. As he recognised me standing in the gloom of the doorway, a smile broke on his broad round face. We greeted and settled into chat. He told me his tale of woe. He had been on time for his plane at Dublin. There was no mistake on his ticket. But all his luggage had gone missing and had still not turned up, even as he leaving his hotel in Brussels to make his way to Ardensberg.

The weather was cold. As we boarded the bus, it was spitting flakes of snow. Ardensberg is just inside the Belgian border; in no time, we were approaching the Folk High School. As we entered the building, we were greeted by a man who, as he shook each person's hand, shouted over his shoulder, "Coffee Nettie, coffee Nettie!" – a refrain we would become quite familiar with.

After coffee, he introduced himself as the course director. He then opened the proceedings by asking us all to say something about ourselves and the organizations that we represented. It quickly became obvious that most of us delegates spoke English, as either our first or second language. In fact, many of the delegates were from Britain. Myself, Joe and two others represented the Irish Republic. There were also two delegates from Northern Ireland and six from Scotland. At this time, the Troubles in the North were at their height. The course director and staff looked forward with some trepidation to the arrival of separate delegations: one from the Republic and another from the North. Like all those who did not hail from either part of the island of Ireland, they had a very fractured vision of a land of continuous conflict, a picture played out night after night on their TV screens.

Joe and I made contact with the Northern delegation early on. We found both members personable and agreeable. If there were tensions within the conference as a whole – a slight unease must be admitted to – then it wasn't caused, as might have been feared, by the mutual hostility between two major tribes on the island of Ireland. Rather, the cause of tension was the leader of the English delegation. Many of the delegates from the regions resented the haughty manner in which he treated them.

During a discussion on organisation and leadership, he infuriated everyone with his use of the gavel. This was typical of him, always conscious of his authority – or lack thereof. At one stage, relations within the English delegation became so strained that he came to Joe and asked him whether we had any hang-ups regarding the English. Assured that we hadn't, he asked for our help in dealing with the tense situation. Amidst all the subterranean tension, the director cried out, "Nettie, a coffee please!"

The course seemed to move between earnest discussion and field trips, three of which I remember vividly. One was to a riding school. The second was to the HQ of the municipality that governed the seven united hamlets. Here, we were treated to sweet sherry and St Nicholas Staff. The almonds in the latter and the sweet sherry made for an interesting combination of taste. After the reception, the mayor delivered a lecture on the administration of his Seven Hamlets. For me, the whole idea of united hamlets was somewhat incongruous. In the first place, the municipality HQ seemed, for all the world, like a diminutive Liberty Hall.

The formalities completed, we were bussed into Middleburg, a large town, the size of Drogheda, on the opposite side of the inlet to the hamlets. At the far end of the inlet was situated the town of Ostend, the principal ferry depot of Belgium and its most northerly port. As we wandered round Middleburg, we became ever more conscious of its size. In Ireland, it would have been classified as a small city. We would learn later, during the conference, there many large towns and small cities in Holland and Belgium.

On the third such field trip, we visited the coast to have a look at Holland's famous dykes. My desire to catch a sighting of them was great since, like every Irish schoolboy, I had been told the story of brave little Dutch Peter. Seeing the sea trickling through a hole in the dyke, Peter had stuck his finger in it to keep the water at bay. Though it was only a small hole he eventually had to insert his entire hand and wrist to try to stop it. Still the water kept flowing. Eventually he had to insert his whole arm up to his armpit.

The school director had made many references to little Dutch Peter. All this filled us with immense expectations about seeing the dykes for ourselves. So here we were in a minibus, hired by the Folk High School, to take us down to a beach where we could judge the famous dykes for ourselves. Most delegates had no idea what they might see, only a burning expectation that it would be quite novel.

Would we be disappointed? We certainly did not expect to be. At last, the minibus carrying us drove onto the beach and down to the water's edge. We disembarked and re-assembled at a spot looking up the beach towards a wooden shop and the rows of sand dunes that seemed to stretch for miles. The beach was ordinary and unspectacular. We were ushered towards the shop that looked like an alpine chalet, and further on towards the sand dunes.

The director kept regaling us with stories of a stormy night that coincided with a particularly high tide. He and all the able-bodied adults in his hamlet had come out to stick bamboo rods in the sand dunes, in an effort to stabilise them and thus save the Seven Hamlets.

When we reached the top of the dunes and looked to our right out to the water's edge the beach seemed very high, especially when we glanced inland. The dunes fell away to what looked like a deep valley. These were the dykes and they did not disappoint us. Then, facing inland, we could see the Seven Hamlets away at the other side of the dunes. The hamlets appeared as small clusters of houses in the distance. Looking towards the water's edge, the beach and incoming tide appeared relatively higher than the distant hamlets. Looking inland again, our eyes rested on the diminutive world that was the hamlets. Down at the foot of an incline, tiny houses were clustered in seven groups. This experience revealed for me the truth of the Dutch dykes, something far removed from the image of brave little Peter, with his finger in the hole, desperately trying to stem the tide.

The conference at Ardensberg ended happily enough but the journey home saw some disruption to my travel plans. This time, the weather was to blame. I arrived at Brussels airport only to discover that fog had closed every airport on the coast of Holland and Belgium. As no planes could land or take off, I had to stay put. Over the tannoy, we were assured that when the fog lifted, we could take our flight. But instead of lifting, the fog seemed to intensify. So we waited and waited until finally, we were told that we were to be bussed to the nearest fog-free airport – Schiphol, Amsterdam. When my plane eventually took off for Dublin and the stewardess came down the aisle offering complimentary drinks, I ordered a double whiskey and relaxed back into my seat.

My time in Macra eventually came to an end. I returned to attending my nursery – and to my seat on the IFA County Board. Through Macra, I have made many valuable friends in the fields of horticulture – especially nursery stock production – and farming politics. I had served, after all, on the Advisory Council of the horticultural section of the Agricultural Institute.

Back in Meath, I became very involved with the IFA (and later, the Labour Party). It was always assumed that retiring Macra members would join the IFA. Like many other former Macra members, I had another motivation for joining: quite simply, my interest in community development. As we progressed as individuals, so we also strove to ensure that our community would develop socially and economically to its full potential.

I also became quite active in the North-East Fruitgrowers Association, eventually serving a term as chairman. One of the outlets for the production of a range of high quality jams and preservatives was the Fane Valley Co-op, located in Monaghan. A smaller outlet, Newbliss Jams, had been run for years by the Leslie family and was eventually incorporated into the Fane Valley Co-op. It drew its supply of fruit from all over the north-east and the Fruitgrowers Association became the principal body for setting prices with the factory.

I was also elected as chair of the IFA horticultural commodities group. My years as chairman were one of frantic endeavour. At the same time, I had to manage my own business – with an expanding nursery stock enterprise – along with its sales cooperative.

Chairing those IFA group meetings oftimes proved difficult. Debate was robust. Much like Macra meetings, everyone had to have their say. Meetings that started at 8.30pm could last until one or two in the morning. We managed, nonetheless, to struggle through these monthly marathons. I'm told that I made it all seem very easy. We also used chance meetings at the Corporation fruit and vegetable market to progress the business of our organisation.

Being an officer on the commodity committee also meant some travel abroad. These trips were usually to exhibitions, conferences and commercial farms or horticultural enterprises. One I remember is the British Growers Look Ahead Conference. The one that sticks out most is the one held in Harrogate in Yorkshire. This medium-sized town was a spa resort, so there were a large number of standard and boutique hotels in which stands could be erected. The exhibitions were so numerous, they were spread all over the centre of town. It seemed that there was scarcely a hotel of any size that had not turned its ground floor into an exhibition space.

All sorts of horticultural equipment were on display at diverse venues. This equipment spanned a range of products: from various sorts of packaging to commercial glasshouses and polytunnels. All the machinery was heavy, mostly large tractor-mounted machines for moving semi-mature trees from nurseries. At the time, my friend, Bob Duignan, was engaged by Tara Mines to plant trees all around the spoil heaps, sheds and reservoirs. Also represented at the conference were various statutory bodies. The one I found most impressive was the Highlands and Islands Development Board. They did a lot of work developing shrub nurseries and forestry.

Another very satisfying experience was our trip to nurseries in the Boskoop region of the Netherlands. This is an interesting region, because all the nurseries are small, even when compared to Irish ones, although the plant population in the miniature nurseries was well above average. This was made possible by assiduous use of chemicals, which in turn brought problems and challenges. One was that the chemicals spread on the ground tended to leak into the canals that were used for irrigation. The consequence was a dangerous build-up of salts in the soil and water.

The most striking thing about the Boskoop system was that those small pieces of ground should produce so much. The co-op chairman who ran the nursery collective did his best to explain the system. It was very involved and required much attention to detail. Much measuring of soil, water and ground was involved. Yet, we marvelled at the industriousness and ingenuity of the Dutch. All this proved very instructive but we eventually had to bid farewell to our Boskoop hosts and set out for another horticultural enterprise: a nursery that specialised in the production of pot plants called Saintpaulia or, as they are commonly known, African violets. The nursery covered approximately six acres. As you can imagine, a space of this size was very new to us.

It was obvious that the lesson that we were supposed to take from the Boskoop nursery was what could be accomplished by proper management of a very small area. The lesson we were supposed to take from the six-acre glasshouse was how such a large area could be managed efficiently. It was truly an amazing sight to see at every bench, a small army of workers sorting through the acres of Saintpaulia, which came in two shades of blue and one of creamy white. The workers were discarding many of the small pot plants, throwing them unceremoniously into wheelie bins. The ones that were saved were transferred to larger containers.

If the way the enterprise was managed came, to us, as a surprise, then the way it was funded came as an even bigger surprise. The development of this nursery was funded by monies drawn down from the Marshall Plan. In Ireland, we were aware of the plan, for reasons that specifically related to our own country. Because of our neutrality during World War II, we almost lost out on funding. Through negotiation, however, we managed to secure funding that was used towards projects such as rural electrification, reforestation, land reclamation, provision of social housing and hospital building.

That day in the nursery outside Breda, we were also puzzled that an individual could access funds under the Marshall Plan to develop his own enterprise. We knew the structure of the fund was – as far as we could see – a public agency which transferred money to other public agencies. Funds flowed from the U.S. Treasury to the various governments of its Allies and friends during World War II. These were meant to aid the re-building of infrastructure, so seriously damaged during that conflict, including ruined cities and transport systems.

The owner of the glasshouse informed us that he had paid back the last instalment of his loan just the previous year. The plan was, therefore, still alive in 1987.

Chapter Eight:
Back to School

The next journey that I was about to undertake was to be one of the most daunting of my life. Usually, I would make a decision and carry it out without regard to its feasibility. This attitude to life normally served me well but this decision to re-enter education at the age of over 50 caused me, for the first time in my life, to harbour self-doubts. The year was 1989.

The night before I left for Dublin and the pre-university course, I could not sleep. The course was to take place at the National Training College in Sandymount. My mind would not settle. This was the greatest step I had ever taken. What if the course proved too much for me and I had to retreat in utter defeat? My whole being seemed to be split in two. One side had the feeling that this was a complete change of life and that all accompanying challenges and opportunities would be an adventure, something to be savoured. On the other hand, it seemed to me as if I were standing on the edge of a bottomless pit. That was in the very worst of times! There had been many such times, especially at school where, upon reflection, I experienced overwhelming feelings of angst and uncertainty. Had I bitten off more than I could chew?

Eventually, my body gave way to deep sleep. When I awoke, I found that I had only 10 minutes until the time my alarm o'clock was set to summon me from sleep. As I pushed the last of the fretful night's sleep from my eyes, I could see through a chink in the curtains that the day promised fine weather. Climbing out of bed, I allowed myself a few seconds to gaze out of the window at the backyard and garden.

In the diffused light of early morning, the stone in the walls of the out offices were bathed in a soft pink light. Gulls stood on the weather vane as if to greet the morning. Everything was bathed in this soft pink light, a crimson blush.

Realising the time was passing, I withdrew my face from the window and my eyes from the garden below. I dressed and had a light breakfast. I then set out on my 20-minute walk to the bus stop. The morning was fresh and cool but promised to be unseasonably warm before noon. The edges of the horizon were already thick with blue. The clouds still in the sky were mottled pink. The coolness of the morning and the promise of a fine day were beginning to show up other sharper colours, as the early morning pinkness began to melt away.

On the ground at the bus stop, four plump grey crows greedily fed on grains of wheat fallen from some lorry. As the bus for Dublin pulled into the kerb, the crows rose from the ground on large extended wings, as if they too were expecting a bus, before settling on the road again and continuing to feed away greedily. All the passengers hurriedly boarded the bus. The driver revved the engine to signify the commencement of the journey. The crows and a coterie of pigeons lazily rose about two feet off the ground, before coming down to rest again when the bus did not move. Eventually, after once more consulting his watch, the driver again revved his engine. The bus finally pulled away from the curve. Again, the scavengers reluctantly rose into the morning air.

All the way up to Dublin, the sun played a game of hide and seek along the horizon. Now, obscured by a hill surmounted by a large clump of trees; now emerging to shine its rays across the large rolling fields of corn, ripening in the autumn sunlight. All the fears and uncertainties of the night before had faded, assuaged by the ripeness of the morning reflecting its golden harvest.

Upon reaching Busáras, I crossed the road and caught the DART to Sandymount. This I continued to do regularly. When the weather was fine, I would stay on the bus until it reached Busáras. Otherwise, I would get off at Clerys and catch the No. 3 bus, which would bring me directly to Sandymount Green.

I would then walk around the corner to the Rehabs. National Training College. The Green made a picturesque parcel with its bust of W.B. Yeats in the middle. I was to spend eight months doing the pre-University course. I enjoyed it, as it allowed me to make a number of new friends. Two of my instructors, I recall quite vividly: Patricia Callaghan from Donegal and Sadie Ward from Drogheda. Amongst my fellow students was Flor Lynch, a blind man from Skibbereen, where his family had owned a chemist shop.

In the beginning, I spent one night per week in Dublin but this gradually expanded to four or five. I would stay in the YMCA Hostel, Radcliff Hall in Sandymount and was well treated. A number of interesting people stayed at the hostel, including Fr Philip, a High Church Anglican, who told the story of his once voting for a lone Labour man at Sandymount because he felt that the young Ruairi Quinn needed a vote, that part of Dublin 4 being quite affluent.

The pre-University course was based upon the Leaving Cert as it then was. Those attending were destined for various third level institutions. The idea was that we would take one or two Leaving subject courses. I took History and English, as did Flor Lynch, the student from Cork with whom I had become quite friendly. He and I also took two other non-examination subjects: Philosophy and Psychology. Patricia Callaghan was our tutor for these two subjects. Although we students would be heading for various different institutions, the course was, in reality, geared towards those aspiring for entry into UCD. In spite of my fears and anxieties, I settled into my studies easily. The course was very much issue-based. This had a radical effect on the way subjects were taught. Contentious issues were raised and confronted.

This was all happening around the time of Mary Robinson's successful run for the Irish presidency. Patricia Callaghan, liberal and feminist, was an enthusiastic supporter of Mrs Robinson. Leaving aside the third candidate, Austin Currie, Mary Robinson and Brian Lenihan were fairly evenly matched in terms of voters' support. Flor Lynch and I both supported Mrs Robinson. A number of students from traditional Fianna Fáil backgrounds were firmly on Lenihan's side. They staunchly refused to be swayed by the controversies that were gathering around the Minister and which eventually resulted in his being sacked by his boss, C.J. Haughey. They continued to support Lenihan. Their steadfast dedication surprised the rest of us.

In her soft Donegal accent, Patricia Callaghan dismissed them as "Thatcher's children". Flor became visibly impatient with them. He would give his guide dog, Derek's rein a quick flick. The dog would look up awaiting instructions. If Flor gave yet another flick, the dog would obediently drag him out of the range of the Lenihan supporters, leaving them a somewhat bemused little group.

Derek became something of a babe magnet. Whenever he and Flor stopped at a pedestrian crossing, women would gather around and pat the dog on the head, while gushing their admiration for all creatures like him. Although satisfied by the attention showered on his dog, Flor always emphasised that Derek was a working dog. This was made obvious when another student started feeding sweets to the dog. Flor angrily informed him of Derek's responsibility. When the practice continued, I had a talk to the student but he persisted nevertheless. Eventually, Flor himself had angry words with the fellow in the presence of some of us students who had stayed back after class.

The classroom that we used most was a portacabin at the rear of what was once a large convent school. Another classroom was in the basement of Gandon House – designed by the same architect as built the Custom House. A short time after the pre-university course started, an election was held for two class reps on the staff-student liaison committee. Flor, myself and a fellow from Wexford stood for the positions. The Wexford fellow and I were elected. The Wexford man's success was explained by another student, who emphasised the fact that there were fellow students from his county in the class. Their provincial patriotism had been successfully appealed to.

We two elected reps attended a couple of meetings. The Wexford man then suddenly announced that he was stepping down as rep, due to pressure of work. It seemed that some of his fellow Wexford men had actually suggested to him that he stand down in favour of Flor. They may have originally voted for him on the assumption that, had they not done so, he might not have got a single vote. They didn't want to see him humiliated. Some of the wags in our small student body even suggested that his own vote was in doubt up until the very last moment! In any event, he eventually saw sense and suggested that Flor take his place. So Flor joined me on the committee where he served for the next nine months, the duration of the course.

We students came to know our teachers, instructors and other staff members very well. Sadie Ward from Drogheda took us for English. Under her tuition, we studied readings from *Soundings*, a collection of prose and poetry compiled by Gus Martin. We also studied plays and novels on the Leaving Cert English curriculum. Patricia Callaghan took us for History. The Irish section of the course dealt with the creation of the Irish Parliamentary Party and the growth of democracy during the late 19th century. This correlated closely with the Irish history I would later study in my first year at UCD, notably with the topics lectured on by Dr Donal McCartney (unfairly dismissed by many as a conservative): the foundation of the Irish Parliamentary Party, Parnell, Davitt, Isaac Butt and the lead up to the Easter Rising. The European section of our course began with the failed revolutions of 1848.

We immersed ourselves in the lives and deeds of the great and good – Cavour, Bismarck, Parnell, Gladstone, etc. – in an age of dominant political spheres. It seemed that most European states and provinces had one dominant leader but Britain had two: Gladstone and Disraeli – one on each side of the house.

History and English were always my favourite subjects. You can imagine what a pleasure it was for me to have to read history books every day, five days a week and share the time with English literature. One day per week, we took a subject that would give us an inkling of what a university course involved. Flor and I took Philosophy and Psychology. The study of English and History did not come as a chore, a task that had to be got through. It was always, for me, a pleasure. I read the many books on the course: histories, biographies and literary criticism included. I also read many novels, along with other publications nominated yearly for the Whitbread, Booker and Impact literary awards.

When I first arrived in Dublin and was staying just one night per week, I had to wait in the hostel foyer for a key to a room because I was not staying the whole week. This was the price of renting on a nightly basis. I would wait for Miss Brookes to come up from the kitchen, where she had been supervising the preparation and serving of dinner.

I must say that, all things considered, I was treated very well at Radcliff Hall. Not long after my weekly stays had been expanded to five nights, a full breakfast started appearing before me each morning. Most of the other residents had to be content with a boiled egg or scrambled eggs. On one occasion, I arrived at the hostel after a long study session at Roslyn Park. It was a very cold night with the first light showering of winter snow. I had just plugged in the electric heater when there was a knock at the door. Opening it, I found the hostel maid with an arm full of blankets. She was worried I would feel the cold. To my knowledge, none of the other residents was offered more bedclothes. She held out four of the blankets. "I thought you might be cold so I brought you these."

She then proceeded to re-do my bed. I was so surprised that all I could say was "Thanks", in a whispering tone. The eventual outcome of all this was that a friend from Northern Ireland suggested, around Christmas time, that we should both put money in an envelope and give it to the maids as a present.

The residents at Radcliff Hall were a varied bunch, especially when we consider that the institution was part of the Young Christian Women's' Association and, as such, presumably set up to cater for the temporary accommodation needs of Church of Ireland members, coming to the city to pursue studies at Trinity or, less often, a business career. The Church of Ireland adherents were, however, in a minority. Most residents came from Europe (Eastern Europe for the most part), and included a sizeable number learning English.

One who made an impression on me was a young Spanish woman named Marie Jose. She accompanied a friend who had come to Ireland to improve her English. She was a pretty young girl although not your typical dark, Spanish beauty, unlike her friend who was indeed dark and sultry. Marie Jose had another attraction: a strong inclination to flirt. I remarked to her that I liked her name and that we had a somewhat similar name in Ireland – Mary Jo. A broad smile broke out on her face as she exclaimed, in coquettish tones, that she was like the Irish version, only better.

So the weeks and months followed. Summer came and went. Other students also made an impression upon me but for quite different reasons. For example, a husband and wife from Romania. Nightly, we would watch the breakup of the eastern bloc on TV. The screen was dominated by pictures from Romania, crowds on the streets angrily demanding the dictator Ceaucescu's resignation, followed by another, more regimented crowd demanding that the dictator take action against the "traitors".

Once again, I was privileged to be able to observe the world changing at close quarters. Much as I had once observed at first hand, the decline of fascism in Europe, I was now able to watch – albeit at second hand – the fall of Communism. Indeed, nearly half a century after the end of the Second World War, the Iron Curtain was still seen as that war's unfinished business. One by one, the Communist states of Eastern Europe trembled and fell.

All the while, I continued my studies with a view to taking History and English in the 1990 Leaving Cert exams. For the exams, all the students at Roslyn Park were dispersed to outside centres. Flor and I were accommodated at the College for Blind People, run by the Rosminians at Drumcondra, which Flor had attended prior to becoming a Secondary School student.

The method by which I eventually did my Leaving Cert was quite new to me. The process involved my reading the question, then composing ten to twelve points. Using this as a framework, I would then dictate an expanded answer into a tape recorder. Each answer involved composing about 600 words. In my case, I was further assisted by the fact that the exercise involved some 'public speaking', as already practised in my days with Macra.

The task of answering the questions was not as onerous as I had feared, simply because I had already practised the technique of composition by tape recorder and notes. I had progressed at a brisk pace but without the huge effort I secretly feared I might require. I soon came to understand that any exam demanded an extra special effort on my part. Once again, the secret of my success lay in what I termed mental and physical compensation – finding a faculty to compensate for one you'd lost, or never had.

When the results came out, I was relieved to find that I had passed both subjects with Honours. About a week later, I received notification of a place at UCD in the Arts course reading English, History and Philosophy. Some other students at Roslyn received similar offers: a girl named Emma was accepted to read pure English at TCD; Flor received an offer of a place at UCC, studying English and History. One girl on our course received an offer from Letterkenny RTC to study hotel management.

With the pre-university course Leaving results, I was over the first hurdle in my quest for a university degree. I decided to celebrate by treating myself. Having strolled down to Ryan's Sandymount House from Radcliff Hall, I proceeded to consume a good portion of cottage pie, while enjoying the pleasant thoughts wafting through my mind.

That weekend I returned to Kells, happy in the knowledge that I could relax for the next six-to-eight weeks now that I had gained a place in college. Indeed, I enjoyed my period of rest and recuperation. By September, I was ready to set off for UCD, having first booked myself back into Radcliff Hall for three nights per week. This would soon expand to five nights per week. The hostel was ideal for my studying at UCD, since it was only a mile or so from campus. A bus left from directly opposite the hostel every 15-20 minutes and travelled direct to college.

At the beginning of each week, I would come up to Dublin on the 7am bus from Kells, arriving at Clerys at approximately 8.15am. I would then take the No. 3 bus, which travelled through Sandymount and a short distance down the Coast Road before eventually terminating at Belfield. The rest of the week, I would just cross the road from Radcliff Hall and catch the 51 from outside St John's Church to campus. I made this journey daily, except for Thursday, which was normally my day off. This allowed me invaluable space to catch up with my reading and treat myself to a leisurely breakfast, which, thanks to Miss Brookes and her kitchen staff, was a full Irish. At the same time, I could chat with some of the more interesting residents. After breakfast I would retire to my room to commence my reading, enthused by a delicious sense of pleasure as I worked through the fiction on my reading list.

Sitting at a bench in one of the lecture theatres in the UCD Arts Block, being lectured in History, English or Philosophy was a huge and unexpected pleasure for me. Before going to UCD, I could ask for no greater source of happiness than to hear a discourse on writers such as Dickens, Austen and Trollope, or writers from a more distant age, such as Shakespeare, Marlowe and Chaucer. I could wish for nothing more than to hear about those authors through radio programmes, such as *The Critics* on the BBC.

One of the star lecturers at UCD was Seamus Deane. His exposition of the English enlightenment was inspiring. One of his lecture series was entitled, *Discovery, Travel and the Enlightenment* and addressed such issues as how the mind and sensitivity of the late 18th century were informed by voyages of discovery. At that time, there were still regions of the world untouched by European explorers: for example, the Pacific Ocean. Though South America had been settled some two hundred years previously and despite the fact that Magellan had circumnavigated the globe, the Pacific remained unknown to Europeans.

Professor Deane's hour-long lectures always took place at 3pm of a Friday; so I would have to miss the 5pm Cavan bus that went through Kells. Nevertheless, I still chose to attend Deane's lectures – even though there were other English lectures at more convenient times. The price I paid was to have to wait until 8 or 9pm to eventually sit down to an evening meal at home in Kells. But it was worth it.

I enjoyed reading samples of American literature, especially Herman Melville and Emerson. My greatest satisfaction however, came from reading the works of Mark Twain, books such as *Huckleberry Finn* and *Tom Sawyer*. One of the best essays I wrote was on Huckleberry Finn. I have no doubt that part of the appeal was that the novel captured the atmosphere of a people that lived on the river. Years previously, my brother John, then aged twelve, had discovered Twain's works in our local library in Kells and passed on his newfound enthusiasm to me. Twain's two most famous novels both concerned orphan boys. Tom Sawyer lived with his Aunt Dorothy, who treated him as though he were a son, protecting and feeding him – and laying down the law. Huck Finn, on the other hand, was an orphan with no such support. He was truly king and subject in his own realm. What could be more appealing to a youngster than another youngster who lived entirely without governance, save for the prompting of his own heart or the yearning of his deepest desires.

Another American novel that delighted me was *The Catcher in the Rye*. A very slender volume, it was a novella rather than a novel. It had, however, sold millions of copies. Holden Caulfield, like Huck Finn, was a fascinating character. Both were around the same age.

Other books on our course included the Middle English text, *The Canterbury Tales* and Longland's *Piers Ploughman*. This particular course was presented by Terence Dolan, who is of Cavan ancestry. He informed us that in the counties of north Leinster and south Ulster, the spoken dialect was derived from the English midland accent of Chaucer's time. *The Canterbury Tales*, like its Italian counterpart, *The Decameron*, was a comic work. It concerned a group of people who set off from a hostelry in Southwark in south London, on a pilgrimage to the shrine of the martyred Archbishop Thomas à Beckett. The Prologue is divided into the Preliminary Prologue and the Prologue to Individual Characters (such as the Knight, the Miller and the Wife of Bath). The Wife of Bath had outlived many husbands. All of the characters are more than they seem. The Knight portrays himself as a shining example of Christian valour. Professor Dolan was able to show that, far from acting as a witness to Christian chivalry, the battle in which the Knight engaged was a massacre of the Innocents, equally notorious in the Christian realms as in the lands of the infidel.

This sceptical reading of *The Canterbury Tales* had been championed by a certain Terry Jones of Monty Python fame. Many of the younger tutors were inclined to be quite dismissive of Professor Dolan's claims, to be a close friend of Jones and to have had lengthy discussions with this famous comedian about the Tales.

Piers Plowman, however, is not a comedy. Its subject is a simple man's dream of Christ and the Cross. It was written as a protest against the corruption of the court of King Edward II, a monarch who was living with his male lover.

The Old English unit section on our course included texts that were, in fact, a mix of High German and Saxon: the language of the Saxons, Tutes and Angles. On the page, it resembled the written Celtic language of the Bretons of northern France. The chief benefit of making an effort with this arcane language was that it allowed you to penetrate the mindset of a people who lived in the early Middle Ages. It was, for me, a complete revelation to be able to connect with people of another time – indeed another world.

Other writers studied on our English course included Tennessee Williams, Ford Maddox Ford and of course, James Joyce. The writer whom I found the most interesting however, was G.B. Shaw. Of particular interest was his play *St Joan*. It allowed us to discuss Shaw's concept of 'Prothelic' (Protestant + Catholic) as applied to this particular saint: almost a Protestant in the author's eyes.

I could not believe my good luck being able to hear such high-powered tutor and lecturer-led discussions each day. So immersed was I in my studies that years seemed to be passing in a moment's dizzying breath.

As mentioned, my other major was Philosophy. My liking for this subject was governed by my attraction to the existentialists, notably Nietzsche, Dostoyevsky and of course, Kierkegaard. Then we have the more modern existentialists – the competitors Camus and Sartre. I became engrossed with their discussion of the whole notion of existence. This, I considered to be the most important philosophical question: "Do we exist or are we just dreaming our existence?"

Apart from the existentialists, thinkers I admired included Descartes, Kant, Berkeley and Hume. I admired the rigour of their enquiry. An example was Kant's *Groundwork on the Metaphysics of Morals*, which dealt with our understanding of philosophy's treatment of the whole area of ethics, in both a logical and systematic way. Although *Groundwork* is a very slender volume, his argument is thoroughly thrashed out. This volume served as a prelude to his great work *The Critique of Pure Reason*: part of a much larger manuscript of his and the last word on philosophy.

The course also introduced me to Wittgenstein, a most unusual philosopher. But like all philosophy courses in the Western world, ours was dominated by the three classical greats: Socrates, Plato and Aristotle. Not everyone believed however, that philosophy began with these three greats. A friend of mine, doing her BA as a mature student, confessed that she could well see why the people of Athens might want to put Socrates to death. She found him annoying, intellectually domineering and overpowering. Although I tried to defend the three greats – Socrates in particular – I could well sympathise with her. After all, Nietzsche had branded Socrates a dogmatist and championed instead, the tragic poets as the great thinkers of Greece.

The years at college passed all too quickly and without the pressure I had feared. In fact, the lecturers and tutors were all too willing to help. Looking back on my college experience, it was obvious that I was given all the help needed to achieve the results required to do postgrad studies. Doubtless, one reason for the favourable treatment I received was that I was a person with a disability. The lecturers and tutors were all too conscious that, with a disability, one might experience certain impediments, preventing one from achieving one's full potential. One such impediment was putting thoughts down on paper in order to answer the questions on the exam paper. Whenever I did an exam, I had the assistance of an amanuensis (someone appointed to write or type what another dictates) who was a pleasant young man impressed with my ideas. The practice was something I had learned from my year at Roslyn Park, and developed during my time at UCD.

One way in which I learnt to use the amanuensis was to write down that which I wished to say in point form. I would then speak from these points as if addressing an audience with my thoughts and ideas, expanding on each point and filling in the gaps. This practice was nothing new to me. After all, it was the way I used to compose my responses in debates with Macra.

Another advantage of an amanuensis was that the scribe could be used as a sounding board. Facing into two weeks of exam papers could be a daunting prospect. All questions on the exam papers were issue based and the answer was supposed to be about 600 words in length: that is, a small essay in itself. As I called out the answers from the notes prepared, I would watch my scribe's face for a response. I must say, he never failed me. I had the same scribe for each of my early exams. A rapport was soon built up and we became friends. Thanks to this procedure, I could tell whether I was being effective in answering the questions on the exam paper. I felt confident I would do well. After answering the last question on the last paper, I gathered up the various scraps of paper and put them into an envelope. Once again, I strolled down to the Sandymount House for a celebratory dinner, before setting off back to Kells, to bide my time until the results came out.

I was so confident I would pass my finals that I did not spare a single thought for the completed exams. Then, one day in early autumn, I set off for UCD in good spirits to view what other students called the "dreaded walls" in the middle of the Arts concourse. I found my name, with difficulty, in one of the many A4 pages affixed to a wall. I found that I had passed with Honours, sufficient to enable me to do a Masters. I applied to do a postgrad degree in either Philosophy or Film Studies, my preference being for the latter. My family had shares in the local cinema in Kells and I was interested in film production.

I was accepted for the Masters in Film Studies. I decided that, instead of trying to complete the Masters by course work in one year, I would do it part-time over two years. This meant that the degree would take two years to complete. During this time, I would get the opportunity to travel to Berlin and live there for a spell to research my thesis, the title of which was, *The Films of the Weimar Republic*. In fact, the college ended up subsidizing my travel.

Chapter Nine:
The Wanderlust – On My Travels Again

I had only to attend college for two lectures per week, each on separate days. I chose Tuesday and Wednesday with an overnight stay at Radcliff Hall. This was made easier by the fact that lectures began at 12 noon. I did not have to rush to college immediately after breakfast to be seated in a lecture theatre for 9am. The lecture in Film Studies was held in a large room on the first floor of the Arts Building, next to the film library where lecturer, Dr Harvey O'Brien's girlfriend was in charge. The only text we had to buy was one by Pamela Cook that students called "the cook book". It covered the entire history of world cinema. It seemed that every film ever made got a mention, space allotted depending on the film's importance. *Citizen Kane*, for example, had two or three pages to itself while more obscure films earned only a short paragraph.

Although I no longer spent most of the week at Radcliff Hall, a full Irish breakfast was still put in front of me every Thursday morning. Needless to say, it was never refused. The fact that I had not to be at UCD until 12 noon allowed me to engage in lively conversations with other guests.

As mentioned briefly, Radcliff residents came from all over Europe, especially Eastern Europe. Most prominent were those from Romania and Bulgaria. The Romanians had fled their country's government. When congratulated on the fall of Ceaucescu, a Romanian couple retorted, "What change is there? Only the chief criminals have gone. The same old crowd are still in power."

Spaniards were also prominent, mostly young women learning English whilst on a gap year.

So life progressed, with me now attending college two half-days per week, all taken at a leisurely pace. My trip to Berlin had been postponed for a year. Meanwhile, I was able to watch all my favourite movies, including the work of Ingmar Bergman. I was even lucky enough to see other prominent filmmakers, such as Gregory Peck and Martin Scorsese, come to address us students in college.

The two years I spent on the part-time Masters turned out to be very eventful. One of my fellow students was Orla Guerin, who had recently run, unsuccessfully, for election to the European Parliament. Previously an RTÉ correspondent in the former Yugoslavia, she is now Middle East correspondent for the BBC. Another student was Ger Philpott, an RTÉ radio producer, who did the scriptwriting module with me as part of a course presented by the screen-writing school.

Yet another celebrity who shared his experience with us was one Eoghan Harris, a very controversial personality with a reputation for being both irascible and unpredictable. Harris gave us a lecture on storytelling, relying on the classic idea of a plot. His exposition of the Greek storytelling idea I thought brilliant, as did most of my classmates. At the end of his lecture the applause was long and loud, which quite obviously pleased Harris, as he graciously accepted his due.

But another side of Eoghan Harris emerged when he spotted a former RTÉ colleague of his in the audience. He made some sarcastic remarks that I was later to learn, hurt Ms Guerin very much. She was, however, accompanied by a young bespectacled fellow who appeared to be a friend of hers. As far as I can remember, he was also doing a Masters in Film Studies. This young man warned the rest of us against taking Harris on in debate, insisting that he was a bully who would doubtless wipe the floor with anyone who challenged him.

These warnings were, no doubt, soundly based. I was, however, to discover an entirely different side to Harris. As it so happened, we were both invited to a talk to be given by the celebrated Scorsese. Afterwards, we would have an opportunity to mingle with the great director and his friends. The room in the UCD Arts Faculty was, however, deemed much too small for those who wished to attend so the venue was changed to nearby Carysfort College, which UCD had brought some years previously, in one of the deals facilitated by the late C.J. Haughey.

Getting to the hall in Carysfort involving crossing a rough patch of grass that was being redeveloped as a carpark. This presented me with no problems on the way in. I just had to take it very slowly and carefully, watching every step. On the way out, however, problems were posed by the fact that the ground to be traversed was on a fairly steep incline. There was also a crowd of people on either side of me. Although I tried to proceed carefully, I was far less surefooted than I should have been. My predicament was exacerbated by the fact that I was now forced to move with the crowd, rather than at my own pace. Mr Harris grasped my situation, directed himself to my side and proceeded to guide me down to the roadway.

The experience of studying for the Masters was different in so many ways to studying for the basic BA degree. It was far less pressurized. It also left enough time for leisurely reading. On the very first day, I was elected class rep on the staff-student liaison committee for the students doing the two-year Masters course. This gave a great boost to my self-esteem – as if I needed it – at this time. Such periodic boosts to my confidence have nurtured me throughout life. They have reminded me that where there is a will, there is a way.

It was in this relaxed state of mind that I began to plan my study trip to Berlin in the summer of 1995. This was a major venture. I feared anything could go wrong: for example, the necessary written texts might not be readily accessible in Berlin itself. The information might be scattered well beyond Berlin, beyond Germany even. As a result of the carpet-bombing by Allied forces during World War II, some of the most important sources had been destroyed. Where in Berlin was the most profitable place to search? I had no idea. A lifetime of coping, however, had placed into my brain and hands the necessary tools for overcoming such hurdles.

When the time came around to set out on my journey, I did so in a very positive frame of mind. I departed Dublin on a flight to Amsterdam, where I had a wait of at least two hours before I could board my plane for Berlin. On arrival in Berlin, I hired a taxi to take me to rooms I had rented, at an address just off Schiligestrasse. I was looking forward to a rest after my long journey – before undertaking an initial tour of the neighbourhood of Kreuzberg. Alas, things were not to prove so simple. Upon arrival at the address, I was met by a rather large, suntanned hausfrau, who was almost beetroot red through over-exposure to the high summer sun. She curtly informed me that I had not written to inform her of my intended arrival and then closed the door in my face.

Although I had travelled widely in Western Europe – including West Germany – I was a stranger to Berlin. Here I was in an unfamiliar city, wandering down the street at 10 o'clock at night. As I proceeded in a fog of apprehension and bewilderment, a number of tramps and vagrants were beginning to settle for the night, taking up places on street benches and crouching at doorways.

It was then that I spotted a sign advertising accommodation. This turned out to be a commercial hotel named Die Fabrik (the factory). I entered the building and approached the reception desk, where I explained my predicament to a receptionist who seemed not to understand. As I turned to leave, I felt a firm hand on my shoulder. A man who I would later get to know as Richard Seimans took me aside.

"Come with me," he said in a softly modulated tone.

"What have I done?" flashed through my mind, though I did not say anything.

Richard guided me up a flight of concrete stairs and into a medium-sized room containing three beds. Confused though grateful, I held out my wallet containing the bankers' orders for the room originally booked.

"How much?" I asked.

"Not now," said Richard, "We shall fix up in the morning."

And with that, he was gone.

Despite the excitement of the previous few hours, I settled down to a good night's sleep. Over coffee the next morning, I talked things over with the staff and other hotel guests. One of the receptionists remarked of herself and her colleagues, "We are not really Germans you know, we are Berliners!" Another took it upon herself to phone my would-be landlady. Meanwhile, guests offered me all the knowledge I might need to negotiate my way around Berlin, especially the U-bahn and S-bahn. The receptionist eventually told me I could return to my original accommodation, if I so wished. I had no hesitation in refusing the offer. Why should I go back to a place where I knew I would only feel alone in a big city – even if the bankers' orders had been made out to that particular landlady?

For the next three nights, I slept in the three-bed room in Die Fabrik. On the fourth night, I moved into a 40-bed dormitory, mainly for financial reasons. This would allow me sufficient funds for my six months in Berlin. This proved to be an interesting time, during which, I came to be something of a celebrity amongst the young backpackers from Canada, the USA, New Zealand and Australia. I was something to be marvelled at: a 56-year-old in a kind of Tir na nÓg. Many of the backpackers were on a gap year. In a rapidly fragmenting world, their first port of call was the breached and shattered Berlin Wall. In fact, part of the wall once ran through what was a park not far from Die Fabrik. All that remained now, however, was a watchtower bearing the inscription, 'Der Museum die Verboten Kunst' (The Museum of the Forbidden Culture).

On the other side of the river, there was a still intact section of the wall. Behind it, many groups of European Romany had set up camp, doubtless drawn to Berlin by the availability of paid employment, especially in the eastern section of the city. Along this section of the wall was a whole series of murals. One in particular would later become famous. It portrayed the kiss of greeting between Brezhnev and Honecker. This image had been based upon a press photograph of the two latter-day Stalinists, on the occasion of Brezhnev's visit to Berlin in 1979.

Wandering around Berlin, one encountered the various epochs through which the city had passed – unlike other capital cities, which seemed to develop initially at a steady pace, until reaching an optimum size and settling down into being the largest and most significant city in whatever country it was. Berlin was different. Each period ushered in a new spate of development, as it progressed from the Hollenzollerns and their golden domes, to the Empire and through the hectic Weimar Republic: War, Triumph and Defeat, finishing up as a divided city! Then came the period of rebuilding and the forest of cranes, amongst which I now stood.

Dublin was undergoing a period of rapid building and development at this time. Berlin however, especially the eastern section, far surpassed anything taking place in the Irish capital. Along with the forest of cranes were cement lorries, which jostled through the everyday traffic of the city. Amongst these lorries were the orange-coloured, Readymix cement mixers familiar on Irish roads, their giant barrel-shaped receptacles revolving at the rear of the cab.

About two weeks after I had arrived at Die Fabrik, Richard Siemens came and told me that I was one of the nicest guests they had ever had. They would not ask me to pay any more rent. I felt a great burden lifted from my shoulders. I could now count on going to bed at night and enjoying the strongly evocative sounds of the Muslim call to prayer drifting in the window of the hostel dormitory.

One day, a group of us hostellers were sitting on the furniture outside Die Fabrik. Otto, originally from East Germany, informed us of his longing for bananas. This reminded me of my mother, who in the years immediately following the Second World War kept a hank of greenish bananas, which she hid behind the sofa in the drawing room, doling them out to us children on special occasions as they ripened. I also recalled the day when, to my surprise, as I was passing Mrs McGarry's shop window in Kells, I had recognised a fruit, roughly the shape of a banana, though much bigger than any my mother had. Like Otto, I had wanted to possess this particular item for myself. All oppressed people must love bananas!

One of the young people who befriended me in Berlin was a young Canadian of Italian extraction named Andrew Ius.

"Could I tag along with you?" Andrew asked one day.

"Certainly, I would be glad of the company."

We set off for the German film studios outside Berlin, in which some of the great pre-War films had been made, along with the former East German regime's feature films and most of their television programmes. Andrew exhibited a great interest in the *Triumph of the Will*, a film that to me was pure propaganda. The documentary I really admired was *The City that Never Sleeps*, an impressive film that caught the atmosphere of Berlin between the two wars. Andrew soon became an aficionado of the film too. We both recognized the various stations on the S-bahn – such as Alexanderplatz and Friederichsplatz – that featured in it.

On another outing with Andrew, we went to see the Brezhnev/Honecker mural. Like me, he recognized its origins from press photographs. Yet another day, Andrew suggested some exploration in and around greater Berlin, beginning with a popular bathing lake. The day was very warm and the sun shone relentlessly on the narrow gravel path leading down to the water's edge. A crowd was beginning to gather. Many of the swimmers were already undressed and in the water, while sun worshippers were in the process of undressing. Some were even applying Factor 12 to their milky white skins. This was a nudist beach – of that there could be no doubt!

One worshipper – a tall, strikingly handsome young woman – had arrived already. She nonchalantly undressed. She was accompanied by a young, partially-clothed man who was applying sunscreen to her pink skin. As the crowd on the slope grew, we lost sight of the couple until very late in the afternoon. By then, the woman had turned a deep shade of pink, which would be transmuted into light bronze. Like the rest of the crowd collected on the slope, she dressed and left the scene. By this time, so too had most of the swimmers and sun worshippers.

Another of my destinations in my travels was Potsdam. On leaving the S-bahn station, directly facing me was the dome of the garrison church of the Hollenzollerns, once the ruling family of Prussia and later, Germany. In spite of two World Wars, occupation and partition, the influence of old Prussia was evident everywhere. Before you came to the garrison church however, you passed what was once the royal stables of Frederick the Great and his Prussian antecedents, now a restaurant and film museum. I entered the restaurant foyer hoping to have lunch while also doing some useful research. All along the restaurant walls were 'ancient' film cameras, large and awkward. In a corner was a shop selling posters and film memorabilia. To one side of the foyer was a café and on the other, a large room that served as the main exhibition space for the museum. It was divided into sections, each of which had a small screen showing clips of classical German films, such as *The Blue Angel*, *Maidens in Uniform* and of course, *The City that never Sleeps*.

The museum proved very helpful, putting a room at my disposal and supplying all the necessary information in English on the film industry of the Weimar Republic. I studied here for the next couple of weeks until I really had to head on to Neubabelsberg, the next station to Potsdam heading back towards Berlin. The studios at Neubabelberg had been established in 1918, to provide facilities and training for filmmakers in Imperial Germany, an initiative of General Ludendorf and the German High Command. The studios did, in fact, increase the production value of German film, just as Ludendorf had envisaged.

These films, with their superior production values, became popular with audiences in the occupied territories. I had been able to get such a wealth of information from the film museum and was optimistic about uncovering a wealth of new material at the Neubabelsberg studios. In this, I was sadly to be disappointed. There proved to be no embarrassment of riches. In fact, there was not one surviving film – despite the fact that the original buildings had been preserved. Nor did any film props or archival material of any kind survive. Furthermore, the great enveloping glasshouse of which I had read was no longer in existence. Disappointingly, the studios themselves resembled nothing more than a Disney theme park – but without any of the German thoroughness. All that was recognisable of the setting for pre-war German film was a number of stone props in the back lot.

After a few months, having completed my mission in Berlin, I returned to Ireland and proceeded to write up my Master's thesis on *The Film of the Weimar Republic: its genesis and its repercussions.*

1995 was a significant year in my life for another reason. Just a couple of months prior to my departure for that historic summer in Berlin, I had moved out of the family house, Doonvarna on the Rockfield Road, where I had spent the first 56 years of my life, and into a small upstairs rented apartment on John Street, in the centre of town. After my mother had passed away in October 1992, at the grand old age of 92, we three siblings had taken the decision to sell Doonvarna. This, and my eventual move some two-and-a-half years later, signified the end of an era.

My return from Berlin at the end of summer 1995 also represented a turning point in another sense. The next twenty years of my life – though especially the decade 2000-2010 – saw my life move in an entirely different direction: into Community Development and, more particularly, an active involvement in the Disabilities Movement, at both a local and a national level. Organisations in which I would come to play a role included the North Meath Community Development Association (NCMDA), People with Disabilities Ireland (PWDI), Meath Disability Action Group (of which I was founding secretary) and the Kells People's Resource Centre. I would serve on the boards of all these organizations.

But that is a story for another day. Suffice to say that these causes became a very big part of my life for a number of years, investing as I did, much physical and emotional energy. I tried, for example, to challenge the accepted place of the disabled in the community. This was hard work but I made plenty of friends and enjoyed my activism during a time of great change – much of it positive. I look back now with a feeling of both achievement and regret: the people like me that it empowered – and the opportunities missed.

Unfortunately, some things came to grief. Human nature being what it is, personality issues played havoc with much of the good work achieved by the various groups and organizations with which I have been involved. Looking back now, it seems that my fellow activists and I were involved in a myriad of such organizations and activities. That was the time that was in it. As a country, Ireland has progressed enormously, especially after our accession to the EEC. We had moved on from my father's generation by doing away with the Poor Law, and proceeding to advance at an accelerated pace of development. Only in composing this memoir did I become aware of the magnitude of my father's challenge to the established way of doing things. As a local government official, he was concerned with social justice. He was very critical of the poor law system and spared no effort in eradicating this injustice. His influence may be seen in my evolution into a Social Democrat, pursuing gradual reform rather than becoming a political revolutionary.

One aspect of my journey has been that quest for mental and physical compensation, to which I have devoted much attention. Here, family counted for much, especially the abiding influence of my mother, the determined businesswoman. One of the most rewarding aspects of my life has been the discovery of unusual sights, that I might have only encountered through books and the stories of Brother Hinchy. One such sight was the dykes of Holland, which, unlike all but one of Herodotus's seven wonders of the world, has survived intact.

One other little insight that I got from composing this memoir was that one recognizes different writers (Chekhov for example) from their distinctive tone and style. This in turn, helps one to recognize and build upon the qualities inherent in one's own writing. All of which assists in the act of composition and capturing some of the highlights of, what I would consider, and eventful and productive life.

This is my story: the story of coping. In life, we all learn methods of coping: not just disabled people. It has always annoyed me when disabled people have been denied that right to cope. For as G.B. Shaw once observed of dogs standing on their hind legs: the surprise is not that they do it well, but that they do it at all!

At the end of it all, I experienced the plight of the ambitious young man; along with the praise I received, I also encountered the jealousies of those who found the going too tough. As I look around today I can see all the changes I have observed in Ireland manifested in my own home town of

Kells, the town where – despite my occasional travels – I am still living after all these years

Appendix
The Star of Abyssinia
by Rex Lee

I have been told of ancient men in the glens
Who never saw the gantries sleep or wake
Across the roofs of man terraced houses
But went to the shop each week in Glasgow's Princess Street.
They followed never the winding track
Leading to bondage,
Or never knew the tyranny of marshalled brick,
The demands of cobbled streets,
Instead, they traced dissolving furrows
In their watery, grey deep field.
The broad sea road,
Their passage attended by foam and sweeping gulls,
Where moments before their boats had crossed.

As colonists and colonised they came;
As colonist and colonised they returned and returned again.
Where singly or in small flotales,
The small ships main their dissolving passage.
Along the grey, deep road,
Armadas and squadrons once triumphantly sailed
And I have been told of Israel's dusky children,
Under a high and merciless African sky,
Attended by birds of prey.
They followed their herds from water hole to water hole,
From cowpath to cowpath.

Unknown to church and synagogue,
They practised the rites of circumcision and burnt offering.
Nomadic jewellers of the desert seeking no promised land,
Hoping for no manna but longing to be fed.

And the mind loves such beautiful fragile things.
The heart longs to find some forgotten valley,
Where sentinel cliffs guard primeval,
Where ancient beasts still graze.
Who would not dare to reach Byzantium's shore
To find a refuge, escaping the storms of time.

Published in *Poets for Africa: anthology for famine relief* edited by Lynda Moran (Navan, 1986)